PROCLAIM *me*

A SPIRITUAL AWAKENING

CRYSTAL CATTABRIGA

Crystal Cattabriga Publishing LLC, Georgia

Paperback ISBN- 979-8-9900588-5-9

Paperback ISBN- 979-8-9900588-6-6

Library of Congress Cataloging-in-Publication data is available.

Matthew 28:19-20,

"Go, therefore, and make disciples of all nations, baptizing them in the name of the Father and of the Son and of the Holy Spirit, teaching them to observe everything I have commanded you. And remember, I am with you always, to the end of the age.

Chapter 1

Prayer

Father God, we approach you asking for extraordinary strength to immerse ourselves in your eternal Word— the sole truth grounded in heaven. Please grant us understanding and insight. Lord, uncover any hidden truths and bring them to our awareness. I ask you to remove any unseen chains and heavy burdens, laying them at your feet. Let them stay on the ground through your words and promises. We pray in the powerful name of our returning King, Lord, and Savior, Jesus Christ. Amen.

CHAPTER 2

A SURRENDERED LIFE

A surrendered life can lead to unexpected acts by God, making obedience all the more crucial. You cannot predict what God might accomplish through your surrender and obedience in life. Some of you have not yet unlocked your full potential. Your choices will shape your family's legacy for generations to come. I pray this book enhances your relationship with Jesus Christ. Strive to be faithful disciples, not just church attendees.

CHAPTER 3

JESUS

Jesus was born in Bethlehem but grew up in Nazareth. At his birth, children were being murdered to find him, prompting his family to flee to Egypt for safety. After some time, they returned to Nazareth. Located in a remote, mountainous area far from other cities, this village was seen as insignificant. It was plagued by immorality and lacked spiritual connection, almost resembling the lowest city among them.

Matthew 13:54, *He went to his hometown and began to teach them in their synagogue, so that they were astonished and said, "Where* *did this man get this wisdom and these miraculous powers?"* As they hear him teach, they recall reports of his miracles. The locals wonder, "Where does this man get his power?" Having raised him locally, they question how he possesses such authority and wisdom. He didn't attend any school or study under rabbis. He doesn't hold a master's degree or a PhD. So, how is he able to speak like this?

The synagogue was a place for reading and teaching scriptures, worshiping God, and educating children. It served as a model for our practices of instruction, worship, and sharing knowledge, all conducted in the presence of the Lord. Whenever Jesus visited a city, he made a point to go to the synagogue, valuing fellowship with the saints and holding the assembly in high regard. Initially, people seemed sincere and eager to understand, but this changed over time.

This shows that sometimes questions are not truly about seeking answers but about provoking others. Therefore, judgment and discernment during conversations are vital. On social media, skeptical questions may promote discussion but are often aimed at provoking conflict rather than encouraging genuine engagement. Recognizing when to remain silent, respond, disengage, or walk away is crucial.

Matthew 13:55-56, *Isn't this the carpenter's son? Isn't his mother called Mary, and his brothers James, Joseph, Simon, and Judas? And his sisters, aren't they all with us? So where does he get all these things?"*

They acknowledge that his father, Joseph, the carpenter, has passed away, and they recognize his mother, Mary. Jesus was the eldest son in a family with four brothers, whose names are listed here. Notably, two brothers, James and Jude, wrote Gospel letters included in much of the New Testament. Initially, they did not believe in him, thinking he was out of his mind, but after his resurrection, their faith in him increased. James authored the letter that bears his name, and Jude did the same. It is also known that Jesus had at least two sisters, making his sibling count at least seven.

Matthew 13:57, *And they were offended by him.*

Why did they feel offended? Because they have known Him since He was a child and have had a low opinion of Him. To them, He wasn't extraordinary, which caused them to take offense at His teachings and miracles.

People often cling to a particular season or their old self, trying to keep them tied to every version of their past—many struggle to recognize the divine within themselves and overlook their growth. As a result, they try to reconnect by recalling the times they knew you best. But what does familiarity truly achieve? It can diminish respect, decrease perceived value, and hinder genuine admiration.

We often treat the Lord similarly; seeing His image on bracelets and shirts can diminish our reverence for His teachings. Even after years of church involvement, many of us become so accustomed to Him that reading scripture feels mundane. This familiarity often leads us to seek entertainment, emotional highs, and lively worship. Simply mentioning Jesus should elicit a distinct response in you.

We dishonor the Lord when we overlook His true worth, thereby depriving ourselves of His greatest gifts.

Over-familiarity can obscure our perception of Him, much like how many struggle to see Him. In **2 Corinthians 5,** Paul describes that our previous view of Jesus was rooted in worldly, fleshly viewpoints. When we regard Jesus merely as a prophet or a man instead of acknowledging Him as the Son of God, our relationship with Him becomes limited. For many, He remains just a carpenter's son, not the divine Son of God.

If you view him only as a carpenter, he might build a table for you, but seeing him as the Son of God has the power to change your life. So, is He just a carpenter, or is He truly the Son of God? Sometimes, our actions cause others to stumble, prompting us to repent; other times, their offense arises not from our actions but from their incorrect perceptions of who we truly are.

Familiarity can sometimes lead to disrespect and dishonor. The Lord teaches us in His word to honor specific individuals. We are called to honor Him, the Kingdom, and all sacred things. The Bible highlights the importance of respecting the elderly and warns against disrespecting them. We should honor our parents regardless of their actions, as it is morally correct. This biblical principle emphasizes the importance of honoring our parents. The teachings also encourage honoring teachers who exhibit good character and live righteously. **Romans 12:10,** *Love one another deeply as brothers and sisters. Take the lead in honoring one another.*

Hardened hearts develop when you hear preaching but refuse to let the message affect you. They reveal areas in our lives where we resist God. You recognize where you oppose Him, hesitate to give out of fear that every preacher will ask for your money, feel afraid to serve, worry about staying faithful, and are reluctant to forgive. You indulge in life's pleasures, and everyone notices. Do you understand why? It's because dishonest preachers allow you to stay comfortable in your wrongdoings.

The Scripture warns, **1 John 2:15,** *"Do not love the world or the things in the world. If anyone loves the world, the love of the Father is not in him."*

We should detest worldly things like sin, lawlessness, and debauchery—anything that goes against Christ. Reflect on these questions: "Is there anything in my heart that resists you, Lord? Is there anything that feels wrong? Am I holding unforgiveness? Where is my heart shallow? Where do I need to deepen? Why am I fleeing from you? Why do I struggle to connect with the scriptures? Why do I hesitate to give and be generous? What fears prevent me from tithing and offerings?"

Why do I see money as something to hoard? Why do I keep taking on debt and spending more than I can afford? Why do I judge others or be overly critical? Why am I so sensitive? It's important to pray about these inner concerns.

Confess your sins, repent, and seek God's renewal for your heart. Pray for humility, purity, focus, and receptiveness within your heart, and remember to pray for others—your parents, siblings, and those burdened with troubled hearts. Reflect on your heart's condition, acknowledging that you might value some things more than Jesus. Strive for a surrendered, pure, and dedicated heart. Invite Jesus to open your eyes to see His glory and greatness. Scripture teaches that what fills the heart influences what the mouth declares; worries originate from the heart. A heart changed by God can help address personal issues, such as marital challenges and family conflicts, which often improve when hearts are transformed.

There may be areas of your life filled with sin or darkness that prevent you from receiving God's best. These obstacles can block your access to opportunities and new experiences. Some of your desires might not be in harmony with God's plans. For others, your dreams or visions could have become idols; what truly matters is seeking God's will. Why not surrender everything? I often pray, *"God, I only want your will."* Whatever your life's purpose, prioritize His will above all. Remember, you have one life—make it meaningful for the Lord. Pour out your heart.

Pray that the gospel message reaches every part of the world in these final days. We lift this prayer against enemies—sons of the devil—who seek to hinder God's work. Pray to counteract evil, mental assaults, emotional hardships, and family disruptions. Stay firm in supporting the spread of the gospel and resisting malevolence. If you're feeling under attack, now is the time to pray. Include prayers for your marriage, household, and to oppose any demonic forces facing you.

Isaiah 54:17, *"No weapon formed against you will succeed, and you will refute any accusations raised against you in court. This is the heritage of the Lord's servants, and their vindication is from me." This is the Lord's declaration.*

We are now in the final days, emphasizing the importance of praying against evil and promoting the gospel's expansion. Pray for God's work to take root in nations where strongholds, false religions, and deception ensnare people. Our brothers and sisters face persecution abroad, experiencing death, violence, and abuse while resisting these dark forces. Let us unite in prayer to fight evil: pray against the wickedness opposed to God's people, seek the salvation of those influenced by the devil, and ask for spiritual victory.

Let's pray for those we know, especially for everyone who has not yet found salvation. Include your mother, father, brother, sister, and cousins in your prayers. Pray for each person you know who might face eternal separation. Remember the parable of the net and ask for the salvation of those who are lost. May our love for

Him surpass everything else, and may He sit on the throne of our hearts as He rightly deserves. Prayer deepens and strengthens our love for Jesus beyond any other attachment.

Dear Jesus, be magnified. I pledge to love You more than anyone or anything else in this world. You are the most important in my heart; You are my greatest desire. You are worth more than all my possessions combined. Let us pray that Jesus is truly exalted in our hearts. Amen.

CHAPTER 4

PRAYER

Dear Lord, as we live through these dark, final days, time seems to fly. I ask that your eternal word's truth deeply impact both your followers and those who do not believe, as they read this. Please grant your people spiritual strength and revival. Tear down strongholds and false mindsets. Inspire those seeking you to crave a deeper understanding of your revelation through your word. I pray that anyone reading this about you will influence others, even just one person. In Jesus' mighty name, Amen.

CHAPTER 5

THE SAVIOR OF THE WORLD

The Savior's hand is on the doorknob, glancing back at the Father, ready to say, ***"Go."*** At the same time, you observe the Father orchestrating global events, preparing for the Antichrist's rise, a one-world government, and a unified currency. Only the blind—those who call themselves Christians yet don't live like one, and those who oppose Jesus—fail to see these signs. You're trapped in your small world, unaware of international headlines echoing warnings from scripture, calling everyone to board the ark of safety before time runs out. Still, many of us are content with meaningless gatherings, shallow sermons, and podcasts that divert us with trivial issues unlikely to matter a century from now.

Nothing in your life feeds into the Great Commission like a tributary. We often get distracted by trivial matters that won't matter in the end, since only what we have done for Christ endures. I hope to inspire as many of you as possible; time is limited. We need to unite as a family—praying, serving, and giving—to do everything we can to spread this glorious gospel and make more disciples, because ultimately, that is what truly counts.

Remember to take your life seriously and avoid wasting it. Rather than focusing on trivial matters, commit yourself fully to serving the Lord Jesus Christ. Nothing is more important than that. The word 'church' or 'Ecclesia', referring to Jesus, does not mean a building. Instead of saying you're going to church, it's more accurate to say you're going to the gathering. The true church consists of God's people. In scripture, 'church' comes from the Greek word 'Ecclesia,' which means 'gathering.'

In **Matthew 16:13-15,** Jesus, in northern Israel, asked his disciples, "Who do people say the Son of Man is?" They replied, "Some say John the Baptist; others Elijah; still others, Jeremiah or one of the prophets." *"But you, **he asked them,** who do you say I am?"* Although it's natural to consider outside opinions about Christ, his followers should have a clear grasp of his true identity. He is more than simply a name in the Bible; he is the one Peter called **"the Christ"**—the anointed son of the Almighty God.

The Lord gathered his followers and entrusted them with a mission: to spread the gospel, disciple others, and nurture devoted followers of Christ, not just churchgoers. In **Matthew 18**, Jesus shares his earliest teachings about community with the future church. This moment is vital because, before sending them into the world, he first teaches them how to live as brothers and sisters. This is crucial because no one would be interested in a God of love if believers are unkind to each other, which damages their witness. Our grasp of God's love is limited if we don't learn to love one another properly within the biblical community.

The Lord, as a wise teacher, first instructs His followers before sending them out with a message. He emphasizes the importance of how they treat one another. In the New Testament letters—before writings by Paul, James, or Peter—all community guidelines originate from **Matthew 18**. This chapter provides the foundation for self-governance within a community.

Misinterpreting this chapter can affect our overall understanding of the gospel because sharing God's word effectively relies on loving one another within the church. Poor community practices can damage our credibility and weaken our message. You may preach Christ, but if you're unloving toward others in your community, your testimony is compromised. For followers of Christ, the credibility of their message is connected to how they live in a gospel community, as Jesus teaches. Before exploring **1 Corinthians, 2 Corinthians, or other doctrines**, remember that the first New Testament guidance on behaving as a church family—whether at Starbucks, with friends, in the living room, or at work—is in **Matthew 18.** This chapter underpins all biblical teachings about community.

Matthew 18:1, At that time, the disciples came to Jesus and asked, *"So who is greatest in the Kingdom of heaven?"* Jesus is teaching eternal principles to prepare them for His departure, but their primary focus is on which of the twelve will be the greatest when He leaves.

They stayed silent because they had previously argued about who was the greatest in their group. Their hearts were filled with ambition, illustrating the scripture that says, *"Out of the abundance of the heart, the mouth speaks."* This emphasizes the importance of truly listening when people speak. Many people do not genuinely pay attention to those around them. By listening closely to their words and understanding what they truly mean, you can better grasp what some of these preachers are sincerely conveying.

We observe that unhealthy ambitions and a craving for glory drive these men. They desire recognition just like everyone else. Many feel compelled to become influencers, start ministries, gain fame, or secure a platform. This leads to an addiction to approval, likes, and praise, which stems from a deep part of us craving to feel more important than we truly are. We seek significance, status, and love from others. As a result, criticism can cause us to fall apart—our entire sense of identity may be threatened because we value these intangible achievements more than Christ.

In His love, the Lord acknowledges their unhealthy, toxic desire for glory, something also within us. Notice how the Lord responds to their question. **Matthew 18:2-3,** "He called a small child and had him stand among them. "Truly I tell you," he said, "unless you turn and become like little children, you will never enter the Kingdom of heaven."

After spending three years with Jesus, they risk missing the kingdom of heaven if they do not become like children. Eventually, a day of judgment will arrive when people stand before the Lord, and He will declare, *"I never knew you."* You've provided services, attended conferences, authored books, and listened to podcasts, yet you've never experienced an actual change or transformation. You haven't embraced the innocence of a child. Because of this, you cannot enter the Kingdom of Heaven; you'll remain outside as a beggar.

In scripture, the term **'turn'** represents repentance in a theological context. The Lord stresses that true repentance requires sincere remorse for unhealthy desires in your heart and mind; He is not just looking for a superficial apology. You might say sorry for your mistakes, but still follow the same damaging path. Genuine repentance means changing your mindset, heart, and life in a new direction. When the Lord reveals your sin and you are on a particular path, the Holy Spirit gives you a choice: to admit your sin and stay on the same route or to confess and turn away from it.

The term **'become'** indicates that a disciple must change, highlighting a universal truth—growth is necessary for all. No one has all the answers. It's important to understand that **'become'** describes a continuous process of transformation. Theologically, this idea is known as sanctification, a gradual journey of progressing from one stage of glory and maturity to the next.

Some people favor sermons that lead them to believe the gospel centers around them. Many churchgoers prefer devotional books and podcasts that evoke warm, gushy feelings, giving the impression that they are wonderful, that Jesus exists to serve them, or that He's like a genie. It's as if they think He will do whatever they pray for, created to meet their needs. In America, this message is standard: wearing a bracelet, asking for something, and expecting Him to fulfill it. In people's view, Christianity appears to be about God serving them, shaped by secular humanistic ideas that have twisted the actual message.

All the letters in the New Testament aim to foster your spiritual, mental, and emotional growth—all directed at helping you mature. Christianity's ultimate goal isn't wealth or fame, but for you to resemble the one who saved you when you pass away. The Holy Spirit's goal in the New Testament is to transform you into Christ's image. Whether dealing with impatience, idolatry, lust, fornication, or finances, His aim is your spiritual growth. Reading the New Testament often feels like a series of emotional and spiritual jolts, akin to exercising your mind, heart, and soul. At its core, the message is about achieving maturity.

The Lord is instructing us, *"You and I must become—I need to be sanctified, and we must be transformed to resemble little children."* **Matthew 18:4,** Therefore, whoever humbles himself like this child- this one is the greatest in the kingdom of heaven.

We often describe earthly individuals as "He's a man of God" or "She's a great woman of God," but what truly defines their greatness? Is it their platform, large following, or talent? Not entirely. It depends mainly on visible aspects of their lives. However, from God's perspective, true greatness is rooted in humility. We tend to admire others for their power and status, but God values character. For instance, a pastor with thousands of followers and a significant ministry might seem impressive, but if his prayer life is superficial, his greatness is questionable. Conversely, a genuinely great person might be someone sitting quietly in the back pew of a church, without many followers on social media, but capable of confronting spiritual principalities and powers from their prayer closet. That individual genuinely embodies greatness.

Humility means recognizing that my worth stems from God and behaving accordingly. He is powerful, and I am not; He is the Savior, and I am not. My life is dedicated to Him—this embodies true humility. Regardless of whether I have a million followers or lead a large church, if I do not see myself as a humble servant and a child of God, I am not genuinely great in God's view. Others may regard me as great, but only He defines true greatness.

The Lord isn't urging us to act childishly; instead, He wants us to embody childlike qualities. The Bible doesn't mention the word 'adult,' yet we are known as children of God. The reason is that adults often become stubborn and resistant to correction, as pride and arrogance can hinder admitting mistakes. Instead, God encourages us to remain humble like children. While logical reasoning can be helpful, preserving a humble, childlike spirit in our hearts is vital. When we all embrace this humility, we can face life's difficulties together and grow stronger as a community.

Matthew 18:5, And whoever welcomes one child like this in my name welcomes me. When everyone approaches the community with childlike humility, we mirror Christ's character—fellowshipping with one another. As we love and communicate, our humility helps us perceive Christ in each other. This results in a beautiful harmony of community where both humility and Christ's life guide our interactions, maintaining that childlike spirit.

Matthew 18:6, But whoever causes one of these Little ones who believe in me to fall away- it would be better for him if a heavy millstone were hung around his neck and he were drowned in the depths of the sea. The Lord highlights that humility is crucial for success in community life, especially in giving. Being childlike also reflects this generous spirit. However, relationships and churches suffer when believers lead others into sin, causing them to stumble. This involves tempting others to commit wrongdoings or having friends who, even if aware of your faults, encourage you to indulge in licentiousness and sin.

This scripture is essential for everyone because our words and actions can harm ourselves and lead others into sin. God hates sin so deeply that He declared it would be better to die than cause an innocent Christian to stumble. Why? Sin is inherently destructive, damaging lives, marriages, relationships, and tearing communities apart. Do not invite, tempt, manipulate, or force others into your sin.

Jesus exemplifies humility and obedience. He descended from glory, demonstrating kenosis by humbly becoming human and taking on flesh. He chose to reveal some of his privileges and, despite being divine, became a man. He humbly washed his betrayers' feet and obeyed the Father even to death on the cross. Now exalted, he shows that the quickest path to greatness in the Kingdom is through humility. To do this effectively and maintain credibility without appearing hypocritical, we must focus on building community. We should love genuinely, stay humble, view life with childlike wonder, and follow Christ's example. It's essential to protect each other from sin, address it proactively, and ensure our actions do not cause others to turn away from the Father.

CHAPTER 6

PRAYER

Dear Heavenly Father, speak to us, your people. Whisper in our ears; exchange our hearts of stone for hearts of flesh. Tear down pride and arrogance, and remove the blindness from our eyes. Push us beyond cultural Christianity and give us spiritual stamina. Help us sit in your presence so we may hear your heart cry out and live obediently to you. May we hate what you hate and love what you love. Let us glorify you always, in your Son's precious name, Jesus. Amen.

CHAPTER 7

LEGALISM

What is legalism?

Legalism frequently poses a serious threat to your Christian walk. Whether subtle or overt, its influence can profoundly affect our hearts and minds, leaving us emotionally devastated and spiritually drained. This powerful idea, known as legalism, presents significant risks for believers. It sneaks into a Christian's life, much like a hidden cancer, gradually eroding us from within. Legalism involves a rigid focus on strict rules and regulations aimed at maintaining righteousness. This view often emphasizes adherence to rules, sometimes at the expense of core principles such as love, grace, and mercy.

We often find laws easier to understand than human behavior, and many have experienced legalism through Christian writings, meetings, and sermons. Many people are currently involved in various forms of legalism.. The initial indication appears when we compare our performance to God's standard of righteousness. We tend to believe that enough prayer results in righteousness, and similarly, that reading enough Scripture makes us righteous in God's eyes.

Another example of legalism occurs when human rules and traditions are treated as the standard for God's righteousness. When we state, "If you're not baptized, you can't be saved," but my Bible shows a man crucified beside Jesus who was never baptized, and the Lord responded, "Today you will be with me in paradise," we highlight a notable contradiction.

Therefore, at least one man in heaven was never baptized, yet legalism claims that salvation cannot be achieved without that water. Romans 6 presents baptism as a public sign of Christ's transformative power in an individual's life, symbolizing the covenant of salvation. Does this imply that unbaptized people are not saved? Although baptism is mentioned in the Bible, there is no verse stating that failing to be baptized will prevent you from entering heaven. These are human rules and traditions. A troubling aspect of legalism is its tendency to elevate personal preferences to divine standards for righteousness.

To clarify, I am not advising against baptism. I am merely stating that if you happen to leave this earth and go to be with the Father before having the opportunity to be baptized, it will not prevent your access to the Father in heaven.

When we treat our individual preferences as doctrine, we can start to believe that those who do not use the King James Version are destined for hell. Personal preferences evolve through exploring ambiguous situations and forming doctrines based on those experiences. Legalism encourages us to create misleading stories about performance or the actions needed to achieve righteousness. Legalism's other consequence is its damaging influence on relationships and churches, which undermines marriages and destabilizes lives and families.

A significant negative impact of legalism, arguably its most damaging, is that it downplays the significance of the cross and Jesus Christ's role. Legalism implies that Christ's sacrifice alone is not enough, and that humans need to earn righteousness from God. That the cross was insufficient. Christ's sacrifice was not sufficient. The blood alone was not enough. Many individuals turn to false religions and cults in their effort to seek God's approval.

When doctrine teaches that the Lord observes you, it signifies he considers you justified and fully righteous, not because of your inherent qualities. Instead, he perceives you through the blood of Christ. I am warranted because my Savior is seated at the right hand of the Father.

Here is an example of legalism by the Pharisees.

Matthew 12:1-2 describes how Jesus, passing through grain fields on the Sabbath, was observed by the Pharisees. His disciples, feeling hungry, began to pick and eat some heads of grain. When the Pharisees saw this, they confronted Jesus, saying, *"See, your disciples are doing what is not lawful to do on the Sabbath."*

The Pharisees aimed to undermine Jesus.

As Jesus strolled with his followers through the grain fields, remember, grocery stores didn't exist. Food was scarce and hard to find in an agricultural society. These people faced daily struggles to survive, and obtaining grapes, nuts, berries, or baked bread was regarded as both a privilege and a blessing. As they faced hunger, God intentionally directed them to a place where their needs were satisfied. This reminds us that God constantly seeks ways to connect with us and meet our needs, sometimes through miraculous means. It might be a check arriving in the mail, a handshake at the gathering, or someone treating us to a meal. I treasure the moment they found a grain field that fed them on their journey. It demonstrates how God looks after His children.

Let me clarify who the Pharisees were. What led to their distress? Why was it important that this happened on the Sabbath, and what is the significance of all this? The history of the Pharisees reveals that a religious group appeared in the 2nd century BC. This group, known for its radical beliefs, eventually split into two new factions derived from the original.

The Pharisees were devout individuals dedicated to holiness, divine commandments, and the rights of God. They considered themselves the primary authorities in Israel, known as the nation's teachers and scholars. For anyone seeking to understand God's word and laws, the Pharisees offered all the essential insights. They expanded their authority and influence, eventually becoming part of the Sanhedrin, the highest court of the Jewish community. As people moved through the streets of Israel, Pharisees were often seen on corners, praying loudly to be seen.

Dressed in long robes and large hats, they pridefully sought to appear more righteous than others. These individuals were the Pharisees. So why were they so upset about the Sabbath? What exactly is the Sabbath?

History shows us that God is not just a cosmic explosion. You didn't come from apes. You didn't evolve from the ocean. It's unreasonable to think that a small dot exploded and now we live a perfect life. Believing that requires more faith than the first five words of the Bible: "In the beginning, God created the heavens and the earth." The Scriptures, from both the Old and New Testaments, affirm that God created our world and established its order, including the sun, moon, and stars, in six literal days. How can we fail to marvel at God's creativity?

The scripture shows that God rested on the seventh day, not because He was tired, but to establish a key principle. He blessed and made the seventh day holy. Therefore, the Sabbath, which is the seventh day, holds great importance. It is one of the top ten laws among Israel's 613 laws. As part of the Ten Commandments, Law #4 instructs: Remember the Sabbath day and keep it holy.

God aimed to teach His people a balanced rhythm in their lives, one that encompassed both work and rest. We all should strive for the same. Being a perpetual workaholic isn't virtuous. If God Himself doesn't model that, He's teaching His children not to live that way. Living out of rhythm shows a lack of balance.

God established the Sabbath so that His people could rest and experience joy in Him. The Sabbath, observed on Saturday—the seventh day of the week—has its roots in scripture, which records that Jesus rose on the first day of the week, Sunday (Mark 16:2, Luke 24:1, John 20:1, and Matthew 28:1). It is a day designated for rest and to reflect on God's goodness. The Sabbath is significant because it is one of the key practices that set God's people apart from pagan nations.

The Sabbath served as a distinctive marker setting God's people apart, along with circumcision—the removal of the foreskin in men. God did this to show people that they rightfully belong to Him. After thousands of years, by the time Jesus came, the Pharisees had introduced a whole new set of rules, laws, and regulations that God had never given initially to His people.

By the time Jesus begins his ministry, the people are exhausted, burdened, and overwhelmed. They are fed up with the numerous rules and regulations of the Sabbath. What was meant to be a joyful celebration of God's presence had turned into a day of suffering.

These Pharisees watched Jesus' every step, constantly seeking an opportunity to trap Him. How does this relate to our lives?

We recognize that some individuals wish for our failure. How many of us have experienced friends who betrayed us by stabbing us in the back and then hoping we fail? Despite this, remember that the Lord prepares a table for you in the presence of your enemies. A powerful way for God to vindicate you is by praying for your enemies, allowing Him to bless you openly in their presence.

We also need to be cautious about false teachings. The Pharisees, much like modern pastors, imposed a heavy burden of rules and regulations on the people, making it difficult for them to bear. Consequently, rather than celebrating this day with God, they focus on avoiding it. Some pastors, apostles, and prophets have issued false prophecies. It's crucial to connect with those who honor the scriptures and avoid those who dismiss the Bible to prevent misinterpretation. Some may cherry-pick a verse and distort its meaning to support their message—a practice called eisegesis. Genuine pastors, apostles, and prophets aim to interpret the scriptures accurately, helping you understand Jesus' and the Spirit's actual teachings, a process known as exegesis.

Going back, the text questions, "Why are your disciples performing actions that are considered unlawful on the Sabbath?"

According to **Deuteronomy 23:25,** *"When you enter your neighbor's standing grain, you may pluck heads of grain with your hand, but do not put a sickle to your neighbor's grain."* This is God speaking through Moses. So, God permitted His people to pluck grain. However, the Pharisees, thousands of years later, claimed it was illegal for them to do that on the Sabbath.

Is that God's law or human law?

Yes, God encourages prayer, but it doesn't specify a required amount or duration. He desires your time and heart. Trusting a man instead of God's scriptures can be exhausting. You have Christian practices without scriptural support, and rather than enjoying your faith, you feel guilty about issues not even addressed in God's word. Instead of reading numerous books about God's expectations, focus on studying the scriptures.

Legalism flourishes when God's word is ignored. Reading the Bible should be a source of joy, not a burden. Steer clear of man-made rules and regulations. If you feel guilty for not reading enough each day, it shows signs of legalism. Your discomfort shouldn't come from disappointing God; instead, it's an indication that you're working on developing discipline.

Example: **Deuteronomy 22:5 states, *A woman is not to wear male clothing, and a man is not to put on a woman's garment, for everyone who does these things is detestable to the Lord your God.***

This scripture has been misunderstood and overinterpreted. Some believe it prohibits women from wearing pants, but was that even an option when Moses wrote Deuteronomy? Interpreting this verse as a ban on women wearing pants seems unreasonable. If a woman works as a construction worker, mechanic, or fisherman, would she be forced to wear a dress? Thank God for your freedom.

If you encounter Christian books without scriptural backing for their claims, it's best to set them aside. Avoid judging their credibility based solely on their fame, considerable following, or financial claims. You should cultivate a habit of loving, reading, and verifying scriptures together with others. While I generally support devotionals, I oppose literature that fails to align with or support the scriptures.

When you turn your personal preference into a doctrine that leads others into bondage, it will ultimately result in judgment for them.

Example: God destroyed two cities, Sodom and Gomorrah, due to perversion. In my Bible, God made man and woman. I'm not implying that I hate people with same-sex attraction. I'm simply saying that everyone, whether heterosexual or attracted to the same sex, should pursue holiness. I can't explain same-sex attraction. I will never judge you for it. I would tell anyone, including singles, to strive for holiness as God is holy. Sometimes, we face various hardships in life. No one turns to Christianity without experiencing pain. What if God never changes your attractions? The only choice is to keep praying to Him for the ongoing healing of your soul.

In **John 10:10,** Jesus states, "A thief comes only to steal and kill and destroy. I have come so that they may have life and have it in abundance."

Throughout your life, you've often heard in church that the devil kills, steals, and destroys. However, when you read it in proper context, the thief Jesus mentions refers to a terrible teacher or a false prophet.

That's why Jesus stated in **John 10:27-29,** "My sheep hear my voice, I know them, and they follow me. I give them eternal life, and they will never perish. No one is able to snatch them out of the Father's hand.

Jesus' teachings aim to guide us toward a good life. By studying and applying them, you can achieve the best life possible. God provided Adam and Eve with everything except the one tree, granting them freedom. Jesus is a Liberator, and life in Christ offers freedom.

I love how Jesus responds to the Pharisees in **Matthew 12:3-8,** "Haven't you read what David did when he and those who were with him were hungry: how he entered the house of God, and they ate the bread of the Presence- which is not lawful for him or for those with him to eat, but only for the priests? Or haven't you read in the law that on Sabbath days the priests in the temple violate the Sabbath and are innocent? I tell you that there is something greater than the temple here. If you had known what this means, **I desire mercy and not sacrifice**, you would not have condemned the innocent. For the Son of Man is Lord of the Sabbath."

He confronts legalism through biblical understanding, not with false doctrines or arguments. Instead, He says, "You hypocrites, how do you have selective morality?" He's addressing the Pharisees, criticizing their focus on the actions of His disciples, while emphasizing that something greater than rules and regulations stands before them. If they truly understood, they would know that God values mercy over sacrifice and desires love and compassion more than legalism.

Stop imposing man-made rules, regulations, and personal preferences on people's lives, primarily when the word of God does not support them.

Jesus said, "If you knew that, you would not have condemned the guiltless—Jesus' disciples." Jesus fiercely defends those he cares about. Jesus told the Pharisees, "I created the Sabbath and I am God from the beginning. I have the authority to adjust it as I wish because I am the Sabbath itself. That's why I can invite everyone who is weary and burdened to come to me, and I will give them rest." Life in Christ is meant to be joyful and free. You should be able to say you are **FREE** and love His commandments. You should feel truly free in Christ.

Paul explains that you are alive in Christ.

Colossians 2:16-23, *"Therefore, don't let anyone judge you in regard to food and drink or in the matter of a festival or a new moon or a Sabbath day. These are a shadow of what was to come; the substance is Christ. Let no one condemn you by delighting in ascetic practices in the worship of angels, claiming access to a visionary realm. Such people are inflated by empty notions of their unspiritual mind. (False doctrine) They don't hold on to the head, from whom the whole body, nourished and held together by its ligaments and tendons, grows with growth from God. (Stay close to the body of Christ) If you died with Christ to the elements of this world, why do you live as if you still belonged to the world? Why do you submit to regulations: don't handle, don't taste, don't touch"? All these regulations refer to what is destined to perish by being used up; they are human commands and doctrines. Although these have a reputation for wisdom by promoting self-made religion, false humility, and severe*

41

treatment of the body, they are not of any value in curbing self-indulgence."

This challenges the restrictions of your religion and legalism. Don't listen to all these false prophets. Not everyone with a microphone, platform, and followers is truly chosen by God. Instead, enter your prayer closet, where the Holy Spirit will reveal glimpses of your future. Love Christ more than anyone else, and hold the scriptures in high regard. The more truths you discover, the more lies seem to remain fixed within your soul.

Desire to keep your feet firmly grounded and your face turned toward the scriptures. Aim to live an authentic Christian life so that your expectations of God are met, as you do not hold Him to promises He did not make.

Desire to love Christ, His word, and His people. Seek fellowship with brothers and sisters and stay connected to the community. Value accountability and aim to love your family deeply. Disciple others and regularly die to your flesh and worldly desires. Be committed to removing everything He has instructed us to let go of.

I'm praying that people will stop condemning themselves every time they fall short. God isn't as angry with you as you might believe. I pray people discover peace through Jesus Christ and choose not to live by man-made rules and restrictions. Instead, let's stay committed to these sacred scriptures and embrace the freedom and abundance that Jesus gave his life for.

No more chains.

No more shackles..

Free yourself.

Free others.

Live in the freedom that Jesus provides, trusting that the Holy Spirit will guide you, just as the Bible is profound.

Do not let anyone impose a rule or regulation on you that Jesus did not authorize.

Chapter 8

Prayer

In Jesus' mighty name, I pray that every chain—mental, emotional, spiritual, and religious—be shattered in your thoughts, heart, life, and daily habits. May you experience a rush of divine freedom from heaven. Lord, deliver us from legalism, burdens, self-condemnation, guilt, and shame. I pray to God that chains are broken and shackles fall because of the lies from those with poor teaching and doctrine. Strongholds in our minds are being torn down. I pray that we grow to love the scriptures, your presence, and the freedom you died to give us. We cherish your teachings and commandments and strive to walk with you in the abundant spiritual life you sacrificed so much to offer. Amen.

Chapter 9

Run The Race

Run the race and then gently fall into the arms of our loving Savior. Not everyone will run that race with the same strength as you—this applies not only spiritually but also physically. As compassionate Christians, we should remind those who may not experience physical healing in this life that they are entirely healed through the Father. This is why we need to live well, love well, and suffer well.

Live in a way that leaves others with good memories when you're gone. Once you're no longer here, only the core of your influence—your enduring impact on others and the love you shared—will remain. These impressions will continue to echo long after you've passed, even as your influence on opinions diminishes.

When we experience loss, grief comes in waves— sometimes accompanied by warm memories, other times shadowed by sorrow. We shift between these feelings, finding solace in Christ even as we struggle with the pain of separation. Losing someone you've shared your life with for many years brings heartbreak and deepens a sense of loss.

The suffering we face is solely due to sin. Imagine if our perfect ancestors in the garden had never eaten the forbidden fruit. Think of a world where sin never entered, where they never rebelled against God Almighty, and where they always lived in eternal joy and bliss with Him. But because of the sin introduced by our pure ancestors, sin entered the world, bringing death and causing humans to feel separation from loved ones. Today, we grapple with feelings that God never intended the human heart to experience.

God did not intend for us to experience separation from loved ones through death. It was never part of His plan for us to attend funerals or to grieve as loved ones are laid to rest. Our human hearts are not equipped to endure such intense pain and sorrow. Sin has caused profound damage to humanity, and the core issue we face is the sin within us. This leads to conflicts, fathers abandoning their families, street violence, single mothers turning to drugs and neglecting their children, and teenagers cursing their parents.

Many trust Google more than scripture. **Proverbs 22:6** says to train a child in the way they should go. (Paraphrasing). Foolishness resides in a child's heart, and corrective discipline can remove it. An undisciplined child brings shame to their parent. This is God's wisdom.

All human suffering stems from sin. Anyone who has experienced insecurity or shame—such as regrets, lost relationships, loved ones, or divorce—has encountered SIN. Sin is profoundly destructive; I have personally seen the damage it brings to my life and heart. I have also observed its harm in the lives of those I care about. Sin has been responsible for destroying homes, ruining lives, damaging churches, and even causing early death.

The human race is tainted by sin. People often see us as judgmental when we challenge false prophets, and when such prophets act freely, we are viewed as not being accountable in the church.

Jesus was the one who looked into the eyes of sinful men and called them, **"You brood of Vipers."** Do you know what kind of sin that was? One of the ugliest sins amongst the people of God. It is the sin of religious hypocrisy that lives in the hearts of people who stand on a platform and call themselves pastors. They preach about a man whom they don't honestly know.

It is a disgusting thing to strap the word of God on people's necks and add legalism on top of that. Turning away your heart is just as dark. Today, many pastors in America resemble that type. In Jesus's era, the Pharisees served as both a political and a religious group.

Some of these leaders sat on the Supreme Court in Jerusalem and held power, overseeing Israel as teachers. However, their hearts were filled with religious hypocrisy and legalism, to such an extent that Jesus later called them "Sons of the Devil." This highlights the tragedy of leadership and exposes the folly of bad religious leaders. Sadly, they are found throughout our country. Christ is present throughout the Old Testament, so there's no reason to discard it.

Jesus often stopped in a synagogue on His travels. A synagogue was a gathering place for Jewish communities. The chief minister acted as the leader, overseeing the scrolls stored on a shelf. Elders had four specific roles within the synagogue. Its primary purpose was to bring Jews together for communal worship. It also served as a place for reading and teaching the scriptures, along with collective prayer. Furthermore, it was used to educate young children.

Many believed their actions would earn God's favor two thousand years ago, but this was due to flawed teachings. You can't earn God's favor through moral good behavior, perfect performance, or legalism. Instead, it is the cross of Christ and His propitiation through grace that grants you righteousness before God Almighty. Understand what Jesus accomplished on the cross: He took your unrighteousness, exchanged it for His righteousness, and made you right before God.

Are you aware of what it means to be a mess as a person, yet God still considers you righteous? Do you understand what it is to fail God both in your thoughts and actions, yet still be viewed as righteous by Him? Do you know what it feels like to fall short every week, but God still sees you as righteous? God continues to work in my heart, and I am so thankful that His blood covers me. Let's be grateful for grace through the cross of Jesus Christ.

You cannot earn or lose His love, nor can you surpass His grace. Only Christ provides salvation. You are justified through the cross, and your only reason to boast is the cross of Christ.

Jesus demonstrates grace and goodness by breaking down barriers for His people, highlighting His divine nature as God in human form.

Example:

Matthew 12:10, *There he saw a man who had a shriveled hand, and in order to accuse him (Pharisees) asked him (Jesus), "Is it lawful to heal on the Sabbath?"*

The Pharisees were always trying to trap Jesus, but even Isaiah, the prophet, tried to free us from legalism when he said," All of your good deeds are like filthy rags in God's sight".

The Pharisees attempt to use a man with a deformity as a tool for their argument, disregarding his suffering and likely embarrassment. They focus solely on exploiting someone's weakness for their purposes. Such actions are deeply sinful and callous. Now, I wonder how many individuals on platforms identify as people of God and preach, yet lack concern for others. Some seek to appear righteous before others, craving approval and recognition. However, underneath it all, they are indifferent to true righteousness.

People who occupy the office of a spiritual leader often neglect human beings. Their focus is on money, titles, and platforms, with some having been under such shepherds. These individuals can be abusive and tyrannical, aiming to ascend a spiritual ladder to reach a mountaintop or position of ministry, ignoring the opportunity to look their people in the eyes and genuinely love them. If people involved in ministry lack love for others, they may need to consider stepping away.

It's like the Pharisees, when they said you couldn't perform healing on the Sabbath because their laws prohibit doing good for others unless they are in danger of death. This wasn't God's law; it was a legalistic interpretation of their laws. Jesus responded in **Matthew 12:11-12,** *"Who among you, if he had a sheep that fell into a pit on the Sabbath, wouldn't take hold of it and lift it out? A person is worth far more than a sheep, so it is lawful to do what is good on the Sabbath."*

Their laws once prohibited helping animals on the Sabbath, but when they saw it affected their income, they amended them, yet they still did not extend this leniency to human lives.

How can you care more about a creature than the greatest being God ever made on Earth? How can you prioritize material things over your brothers and sisters? Why do preachers prioritize a building, a crowd, or a budget over caring for souls? Isn't a human being's suffering more valuable than the tangible things you trust?

Jesus says, "It is lawful to do good on the Sabbath." That is when you have an opportunity to do good, and you should take it. When the Spirit of God urges you to do good, don't wait until next week. You can't predict what might happen then. The ideal time to act is when the spirit prompts you.

Jesus- I want you to show compassion for human beings.

How troubling is it when individuals call themselves Christians but lack compassion for those suffering? We identify as Christians, yet often lack empathy. The Lord is guiding us to understand that His people should embody compassion and surpass strict legalism. Love should take precedence over legal rules. Compassion is the response we should have when others are in need. When the Lord speaks, anything he tells you to do, grace will follow for you to do it.

There's grace to do whatever God calls you to do. There's healing in the word that comes from Jesus. When I hear, "Stretch out my hand," I hear compassion toward others and love for one another. He's also telling you to stretch out your hand and start the ministry, write the book, be healed in that particular

54

area, forgive that person, let that go, and get over that. Stretch toward Jesus for your needs, but then stretch toward others for their needs.

While Jesus faced constant tests, He also understood when to withdraw from certain situations. Sometimes, avoiding unnecessary trouble is necessary, and other times, you must know when to step into meaningful trouble. Jesus could have healed the man with the withered hand the day after the Sabbath, but He took a stand, stepping into the space of somebody's suffering. That's what we need to do: take a stand for biblical righteousness against legalism and false doctrine.

Take a stand for what is right in the sight of God. We can't always cower from every battle. We can't always be quiet in every moment. Sometimes, you have to know how to get in good trouble. To raise a standard of righteousness. To cry aloud from the rooftop and spare not. Why do we allow the devil to control the narrative? Where are the people of God?

Where are the men and women who will stand for righteousness and step into complex spaces? Do not wait until tomorrow. Take a stand for Christ today. Be the voice for the Lord Jesus Christ today. Step into the suffering of people you love today.

Seeing what the Lord has done in someone else's life gives you faith that he can do the same in your life. This was to fulfill what was spoken by the prophet Isaiah. Matthew, who's writing to a Jewish audience, writes his gospel to prove that Christ is the Messiah, which the Jews today have still rejected. **Matthew 12:18-20,** *Here is my servant whom I have chosen (this is God talking about Christ), my beloved with whom I delight; I will put my Spirit on Him, and He will proclaim justice to the nations. He will not argue or shout, and no one will hear his voice in the streets. (Jesus is not arguing with foolish people) He will not break a bruised reed (Jesus will not hurt people unnecessarily), and He will not put out a smoldering wick until He has led justice to victory.* This is Isaiah, who wrote seven hundred years before Christ. **Reference Isaiah 42:1-3.**

In **Matthew 12:21,** *" The nation will put their hope in His name."*

In the name of Christ, the Gentiles (YOU) will hold. Jesus came for the Jews first, but they rejected Him. Twenty-seven hundred years before Christ's birth, **Isaiah 42:4** says, *"He will not grow faint or be discouraged until He has established justice in the earth; and the coastlands wait for His law."* Let the gospel go to all non-Jews, where they will find hope until the tribulation.

Daniel prophesied about this, and John the Revelator wrote about this. We're living in the time of the Gentiles, but God is reconciling our people to himself from all around the world. In these last days, he's gathering men from all nations, tribes, and tongues and putting them aboard the ark of safety. He's going to keep winning the hearts of the Gentiles until he turns his attention back to the Jews in the Great Tribulation. Right now is the era of grace, and today is the day of salvation.

My prayer for you, all who bear the name of Christ, is that you embody love and compassion towards others. Let us reject legalism and seize every opportunity to do good. Our concern should be more for people than for rules and regulations.

CHAPTER 10

PRAYER

Father, you confront us with your love because we are your children. I ask for strength and guidance to understand your eternal truths in your Word. I pray for my brothers and sisters that you will capture our attention, remove every distraction, and teach us through close focus. Grant us revelation, insight, and understanding from your sacred scriptures. May we see Christ fully and stand in awe of the Lord Jesus Christ. Renew in us a sense of wonder toward the Savior. Strip away our familiarity so that even when we read the

Word, we are captivated by our Savior. Foster deeper intimacy with Christ and reduce our infatuation with people. Breathe Spirit of the Living God, breathe on us now. Bring Your Word to life within our hearts, minds, and souls. Let it energize and awaken someone's spirit today. Let us take a moment to marvel at our Savior's wisdom and stand in awe of Him. May we behold Him as Isaiah did—high and lifted up. I pray all this in the powerful name of our Lord and Savior, Jesus Christ. Amen.

CHAPTER 11

GOD'S CALL

Christianity can't end with a Sunday morning gathering. It only helps to fuel our walk with Jesus, and our walk should be more than a gathering. A church should be a House of proclamation and presence, yet reminding you to always yield to the Holy Spirit when He speaks. The relationship between a pastor and their flock, as well as among brothers and sisters, is fluid. Leaders fear letting the Holy Spirit in because everything is so rigid. The Holy Spirit can't even breathe into your schedule. Everything is in and out.

The Lord uses our strengths and our weaknesses. Our mountaintops, valleys, testimonies, and failures work together to be an agent of strength for one another. That is when I am weak, you are strong; when you are strong, I am weak. You're there to pick me up when I fall, and I'm there to pick you up when you fall. When you confess, I will be a shoulder and an ear. This is how fellowship with brothers and sisters in Christ needs to be for one another.

The Holy Spirit is a powerful agent living inside the believer whom God poured out on the world. The godhead leads us into a deeper relationship with God. To awaken us when we are dead and to move in our hearts. Jesus called him The Holy Spirit, The Comforter. He put a definite article there on purpose because there are other spirits. He planned "the" in front of the Holy Spirit to distinguish him from false spirits and some evil spirits.

So it is God the Father, God the Son, and God the Holy Spirit. The word "the" does not diminish him. It is a Greek definite article that distinguishes him. God also uses another word to transform his children: **exposure**. Once you've been exposed, you cannot be unexposed. God will use exposure in your life to usher you into a more profound revelation of who He is and what He's doing on earth, and to awaken you sometimes when you're sleeping. God uses exposure to transform the life of the believer. Exposure comes in different forms. It could come in the form of a relationship in which God gives you access to a person's life, and because of that person, you have exposure now. Perhaps God has given you exposure to a prayer life, faith, or resources you have never seen before.

Sometimes you see things in someone's life that you say, "I'm inspired now to pray at that level, to be faithful at that level, to preach at that level, to sacrifice at that level. He uses opportunities for exposure. God will provide opportunities in various places or cities, using them as a means to deepen your relationship with Him. God will reveal things to you when you're obedient to Him. John the Baptist's ministry was anointed with God's word. He didn't have a stage or powers of healing, yet people came to hear the word.

This new generation of Christians is attempting to walk with God without relying on His revelation. They trust preachers more than the Bible and often can't recognize lies because they lack familiarity with God's Word. Your walk with Christ should be so full each day that you see God in everything: mountain tops and valleys, tough seasons, seasons of blessing, closed doors, and open doors.

What are we going to hand off to our children?

Other countries don't have what we have, yet we take church, biblical preaching, and the gathering of the Saints for granted. Even though people paid the price and blood for you to sit and hear the word of God, you still can't lift your hand to praise God or sing a song. Why? This is why you feel like you have nothing to pray about, because your Christianity is myopic; you have no idea what's going on outside the US. Hence, your prayers are limited to "Bless me, God helps me," but you have no idea what's coming. You don't see the tsunami coming toward America. Eastern religions mandated that they dominate with violence, pushing out Christians. Read about the seven churches in the book of Revelation.

What happened to the church that was there? The church that was born at Pentecost. Jesus was frustrated with the Christians who were in Turkey. Some of that probably ate out the church from the inside. John was the only follower of Jesus from the original apostles who was not brutally murdered and martyred for the faith. He was boiled in oil, survived, and then banished to an island about 20 to 30 miles off the coast of Turkey called Patmos. He was there as an old man when the Lord appeared to him. **Revelation 1:1-3**

He is the one who holds the seven stars in his right hand. That represents the pastors. Who walks among the seven golden lampstands? The lampstands represent all churches. Jesus says, "I walk among you." Nothing is happening in any church I can't see. Nobody is getting away with anything, not even pastors. Everybody's going to give an account. You think He's blind and can't see? He says, "I walk amongst every church."

In Revelation, He (Jesus) instructs John to write letters to the seven churches.

The church of Ephesus- Revelation 2:1-7

A prominent and affluent church in Turkey, known as a megachurch, became wealthy and accumulated many resources. However, due to these possessions, it drifted away from its original love for Jesus. This raises the question: how many of us are losing our first love? When he saved you, you loved him, and you were on fire. Then you receive a little blessing. Maybe a better job, the house you wanted, a car, and now your first love is your stuff. You've made yourself an idol, your relationships an idol, and now, because you're blessed, you could sin. You can do what you want because you've put Jesus on the back burner and have abandoned your first love.

You may have dreams that you idolize above your intimate relationship with Jesus. What if He said no to your dreams? Could you love Him still? What if you don't get married? Could you love him still? What if you don't have children? Could you still love Him?

How many of us could still say Jesus is my primary love? Would He be enough if you had only Him and nothing else? Can you say you're delighted with him? If Jesus were the ultimate source of satisfaction, everything else would be icing on the cake. Imagine your heart constantly exploding with gratitude because Jesus is all you want and need.

The church of Pergamum - Revelation 2:12-17

False doctrine and sexuality destroyed this church.

God tells us that sex is for married people. God does not like sexual immorality. Sexual immorality is killing the witness of believers all around this country. It's killing the witness of the church in America. You think Jesus doesn't care about that. People are indulging in false doctrine and sexual immorality. Some people want Jesus and all of their immorality. This is not to condemn any of us, whether we are struggling with lust or adultery in the heart. This is to awaken us. The church in Turkey was eroded by abandoning its first love.

The church of Thyatira- Revelation 2:18-21

The church of Sardis- Revelation 3:1-6

Be careful; not everything big and glamorous is Godly. Any man can call himself a prophet, preacher, pastor, priest, and gather a crowd, but that doesn't mean the Spirit of God is there.

If the Spirit of God is alive in your church, you should feel the presence of Almighty God being alive. Demons should shudder when you walk into a room.

The church of Laodicea- Revelation 3:14-22

Unfortunately, this is how some Christians behave. They are lukewarm. Why? Christianity is often reduced to just a Sunday morning service; some have no prayer life. If you don't spend time with God outside of Sunday, you have no evidence of Christianity outside of the gathering. Many Christians go through the motions.

Smyrna & Philadelphia were the only two churches Jesus breathed on with kind words. **Revelation 2:8-11 & Revelation 3:7-13**

These things that ate up the church in Turkey are killing us right now. How could He have died for us, and all we got is this apathetic, weak, soft, going-through-the-motions Christianity? We want Jesus and sin. Where is the fire? Where is the sacrifice? Where is the seriousness? Where are the tears that are being shed? What does your prayer life look like?

God is crying out, "Children, live for me. Sacrifice, serve, pray, and spread the gospel."

You can pray and cry out for the church. If the people of God don't take the Commission seriously, God help

America, help our children, and help the faith. We can't be just satisfied with doing a service on Sunday morning. Don't just beg God for stuff when people are dying and going to hell. We should be crying out for a nation that sits in spiritual darkness. There are over 2 billion people on the other side of the world, some of whom have never even heard the name of Jesus.

If a child has never heard the name of Jesus, can't you see that in America, Christianity is being swept out from under our feet? The next generation emerging behind us doesn't even know the name of Jesus. God said, "On this rock I will build my church." He's speaking to all of us.

Matthew 24:14, Jesus said, "This good news of the kingdom will be proclaimed in all the world as a testimony to all nations, and then the end will come."

Jesus cares about the entire world!! So, when was the last time you PROCLAIMED the gospel? When was the last time you prayed for the gospel to spread worldwide? God said, ***"Pray for peace in Jerusalem,"*** in **Psalms 122:6-7**. Are you praying for churches to be planted and for missionaries? Do you pray, "Your Kingdom come, your will be done?"

Chapter 12

Prayer

Dear Lord, we seek a revival and awakening, calling our hearts to repentance so we may fall on our knees and cry out to you. Open our eyes to recognize the spiritual brokenness in this nation. Baptize us with your perfect love. Let us be grieved over those distant from you. Remove our hearts of stone, give us hearts of flesh, and save us from all that you despise. Help us love what You love. Pour out your Spirit on us. Amen

CHAPTER 13

GIVE ME THE WORDS

Deep within, I pray for you to cherish Jesus Christ and the scriptures. We all need to read the scriptures and love His teachings. Over time, God's presence can seem mundane if we become too accustomed to the scriptures. Some people find the scriptures dull because they've known them their whole lives. I pray that our passion for Jesus Christ never fades.

I encourage you to read the scriptures personally and not just rely on others' words. Studying for yourself helps you determine whether what you hear aligns with biblical truth or if preachers are misrepresenting it. This way, you can hold them accountable.

Revelation 1:3, *"Blessed is the one who reads aloud the words of this prophecy, and blessed are those who hear the words of this prophecy and keep what is written in it, because the time is near."*

Many people have theological arguments around what happens in life and after death: neither agnostics nor atheists, nor Christians, nor many other religions agree. There are so many disagreements on what happens to people after death when they breathe their last breath. Those who take their last breath will wake up on the other side and realize that there is one true God and one true Son. Judgment is upon everyone, and every knee will bow. It doesn't matter what religion. Then, we will all agree there was one Lord and one God, whether we knew Him or not. We will all be unified after death.

Will you be recognized in the kingdom, or will you be the one who was so close to God, yet never really repented? Will God say to you in **Matthew 7:22-23,** "On that day many will say to me, Lord, Lord, didn't we prophesy in your name, drive out demons in your name, and do many miracles in your name?" Then I will announce to them, 'I never knew you. **Depart from me, you lawbreakers!'**

You've been around the church your whole life, but never repented and put your faith in Christ. You have little Christian posts, but you've never been filled with the Spirit. You have one foot in the world and one foot in the Kingdom. One season you're with God and one season you're not with God. You've heard the gospel and about the cross so many times, and you harden your heart.

Are you a person who says, "I'll believe God if or when or I need God to show himself or do something first before I believe." I need God to perform for me, or I need a sign. You know people like that. I know people like that. These are people we should be praying for. Some of them are in your family. Some of them are your closest friends. Some of them are your parents. Some of them are your siblings.

Heal my mother first, and then I'll believe Jesus was your son. Change this situation first, and I'll believe Jesus is your son. People demand proof of God's existence. This is the tragedy of the worst group, which will end up separated from God. Famous people preaching every Sunday are headed to hell. Wolves come in sheep's clothing, so we must watch for their fruits.

The Pharisees asked Jesus, *"Teacher, show us a sign."* Despite Jesus healing a blind man and casting out demons, they still demanded a sign. They called him a teacher, but their tone was sarcastic and disrespectful. These Pharisees hated Jesus, envied him, and even wanted to kill him. Essentially, they were asking, "Prove to us that you are the Son of God." This is why we need discernment. Some people will smile in your face and say friendly platitudes, calling you sister or brother, but in their heart, they don't like you. They are hoping for your downfall. The Pharisees weren't the first to attack Jesus' character for who he was.

In **Matthew 4:3-10** *Paraphrasing*- When Jesus was in the wilderness, another person rolled up on him, called Satan, saying, *"If you are the Son of God, turn these stones into bread. If you are the Son of God, throw yourself down. If you bow down and worship me, I will give you all this."*

The devil was trying to provoke him about his identity and make Him do things outside the Father's will.

Remember, you can do good things, but they are not godly if they are not in God's will. The devil and Jesus both quoted scriptures, which highlight the importance of discernment when listening to preaching. Not everyone who quotes scripture is necessarily speaking for God, so discernment is essential even during sermons. This is why you have to know who you are in Christ.

And we have to realize that some people cannot be helped. Some of you might have a Jesus complex, trying to help those who are determined to oppose Christ. It's best to pray and turn them over to Satan temporarily, so their flesh can be challenged. All God needs to do is remove His protection from them.

You must be careful when your identity is wrapped up in everything except your savior. Your identity is in your title. If your identity is not in Christ, then your identity is on a shaky foundation.

Matthew 16:4, "An evil and adulterous generation demands a sign, but no sign will be given to it except the sign of Jonah."

Miracles are not meant to prove God's identity to quell your doubts. Your attachment to everything besides Him is preventing you from truly seeing who He is. Considering His nature, can you believe in who He is, or does He need to perform to win your approval? Are you mad at God for something he did not do that you've been praying for?

Do you feel anger and blame Him for not giving the sign you needed to strengthen your faith during that time or season? You might be questioning if God's love is evident due to the persistent thorn He hasn't removed. Additionally, you may wonder if His love is in doubt because He hasn't answered your prayers in the way you expected.

Example: Jonah

Jonah was a Jew who lived before the time of Jesus. He was a faithful prophet in the days of Israel, prophesying the things of God. Jonah had no problem preaching to his people. Still, later in his life, God confronted Jonah and told him, "I want you to go to a city called Nineveh, which is the capital city of an ancient empire called Assyria." The Assyrians were enemies of the people of God, and they were ruthless. They were brutal, and they would raid the nation of Israel and take their crops and take their heart. They were ungodly pagans; they were far away from God.

God tells Jonah, "Preach to your enemies and step out of your comfort zone to show that My love and grace are for all people, not just Jews." Despite God's command to preach repentance to Nineveh, Jonah boards a ship and heads the opposite way.

Sin will hold you back when you intentionally run away from a sovereign God. Faith that comes with conditions isn't true faith, and obedience with conditions isn't genuine obedience. Scripture describes how God caused a storm to arise on the sea; the sailors on the ship seized Jonah, threw him overboard, and God then prepared a great fish to swallow him. Despite Jonah's rebellion, God remains present and refuses to abandon him. Even if you are in a season of rebellion, God's hand is still upon you.

Have you ever felt ashamed of something you've done, yet God, in His mercy, refused to let go of you? Was there a moment when you thought you'd messed up, but God's reply was one of mercy?

God prepared a great fish to swallow Jonah, saving him from dying in the ocean. The whale then carried Jonah to Nineveh. When you attempt to flee from God, He knows how to create circumstances that lead you back to obedience. Your purpose on earth is so vital that the Lord won't allow you to falter. The task God assigned to Jonah was crucial because it carried significance for that specific moment.

After keeping Jonah in the belly of the whale for 3 days and three nights, God directs the whale to spit Jonah up on the shore of Nineveh. Jonah walks the city of Nineveh preaching repentance, and the scripture tells us that an entire city turns to God.

Imagine the impact of one man's faithfulness: preaching to a city that then turns to God. Jonah's being swallowed and preserved for three days and nights symbolizes how Jesus Christ would die on a Friday and rise again on Sunday morning. The sign of

Jonah points to Christ's crucifixion, burial, divine resurrection, and appearances afterward.

Jesus declared that this generation would only be given the sign of Jonah. Therefore, the only confirmation of my identity will be my resurrection. As we understand him, Christ is the only founder of a faith that was crucified and died, yet was witnessed alive by hundreds in the first century. The Pharisees had the promises of the coming Messiah and were close to the Kingdom, yet they couldn't accept Jesus as the Son of God. In contrast, Gentiles—men and women who never traveled across oceans and had no prior stories or promises—believed more quickly than many who were so close to entering the Kingdom.

Are you seeking proof that God is faithful? He demonstrated it by raising Jesus from the dead. If you need reassurance to repent and trust Him before judgment arrives to overwhelm you, recall: He raised Christ from the dead. We should stop treating God like a wish-granting genie. Faith in God isn't just about what He has done for you; it's rooted in His work on the cross, which is always evident. The power of the resurrection affirms that He is the Son of God and warrants your worship, praise, and loyalty.

No other signs are necessary. The only sign you need is that He is alive and seated at the Father's right hand—if that isn't enough, nothing else will be. Your heart should fill with gratitude, knowing you are loved unconditionally. Rest in the certainty that you are securely held in His hands, with your name written in the Lamb's book of life. One day, you will be with Him, and through His death, burial, and resurrection, you can trust that God's Spirit dwells within you. Hear God's call, which empowers you to remain faithful, and give yourself wholly to Him.

The sign calls us to take the Commission, scriptures, and gospel seriously. We must be filled with God's Spirit, be saved, and fully repent. Avoid trying to make God prove His love—He has already shown His love, worthiness, and faithfulness. His character assures us that the Bible is trustworthy. God raised Jesus from the dead, and if His resurrection isn't convincing enough, then nothing will be. Are you ready to die for the Savior because of the resurrection?

CHAPTER 14

PRAYER

Father God, deliver us from trying to prove Your faithfulness, character, genuineness, and love through tangible things. I pray you will soften hardened hearts and reveal what you accomplished on the cross. Grant us a revelation of a resurrected Savior, because you live, we shall live, and because you live, we have eternal life. Lord, empower my brothers and sisters to testify of you boldly. May we confidently walk into rooms, preach, and stand for you. We oppose evil because you have risen from the dead. Let us not live with one foot in the world and one foot in your Kingdom, for you alone are worthy. Amen.

CHAPTER 15

FAMILY

It is crucial to love and care for those in need, to gaze into someone's eyes and recognize their humanity, rather than looking down on them. Remember, you are a blessing from God's Grace and can't claim credit for what you have. Avoid judging people based on their current situation, as some circumstances are beyond their control. As children of God, we should not remain passive in the House of God, but actively be the hands and feet of Jesus.

Why do we preach to others? What is our ultimate goal for ministry? What are we equipping Christians for today? Are we merely teaching them to ask God for everything they desire, or are we preparing them for the upcoming tribulation? Are we training them to stand firm in the face of adversity and the rapture?

No matter your current situation, you have been saved for His glory alone. Your true identity is revealed through your view of Christ. **(Isaiah 6:8)** 'Here am I, send me.' I dedicate my life to your service. We should value the written word more than men's oratory skills. We ought to be able to read God's word and feel awe without needing entertainment to stay engaged. An open Bible remains the most potent symbol for the church gathering. With time running out and Jesus returning, life is too brief for grudges and unforgiveness. We must strive to live, love, and forgive generously.

According to the scriptures, God—who created the family—is one of society's fundamental institutions and building blocks. The family was composed of a male, a female, and their children. This family unit served as the foundation for teaching human beings about community, loyalty, and shaping mental, emotional, and spiritual development.

Since its inception, the idea of family has faced an unseen demonic force that has manifested in the human world. From the very first murder between siblings **(Cain & Able)**, the family structure established by God has been persistently targeted to undermine both its original purpose and its representation in society. Throughout history, it has been evident that the traditional family, as designed by God, has been gradually eroding across generations. At the core of this decline are two powerful questions.

First, what defines a family? The second question is, who counts as my family? Are there two males and a child? Or two females and a child? Should we marry anybody as ministers of the gospel?

In the broadest biological sense, a family is any group connected by blood, marriage, or adoption, encompassing parents, grandparents, siblings, and cousins. This also includes stepfathers and stepmothers. Jesus radically changed the 1st-century worldview with one of the most revolutionary statements ever made. This moment not only transformed the world but also introduced a new language and perspective on what constitutes a family.

The scriptures indicate that Jesus was born to Mary, a Jewish virgin, with Joseph, her stepfather, who never had relations with her. Joseph is not referenced in the text because of the conventions of that era. It is generally assumed that Joseph had died by this time. If so, Jesus, being his mother's firstborn, would be responsible for supporting the household financially.

According to the scriptures (**Matthew 13:56**), Jesus had four biological brothers named in the texts. Among these, James and Jude authored New Testament letters that bear their names. The scriptures also mention that Jesus had sisters, but they do not specify their names or how many there were; it only indicates "sisters," suggesting he had at least two or more.

John 7:3-5 notes that Jesus' brothers initially doubted His claims, only believing after His resurrection, which convinced them.

Which faith carries more significance—yours or theirs? This shows how one can be close to the Lord yet not honestly know Him. Picture attending church your entire life, believing you're saved, only to find at death that your name isn't in the book of life. You beg God for mercy and realize there are no second chances. **2**

Corinthians 13:5, *Test yourselves to see if you are in the faith. Examine yourselves. Or do you yourselves not recognize that Jesus Christ is in you? - unless you fail the test.*

When someone says, "I tried Jesus and he didn't work for me," it indicates they were not genuinely saved. What they went through was simply a matter of religion.

Jesus' family believed he was out of his mind. His townspeople thought he was crazy, and privately, his family might have wondered, "Why is my brother walking around claiming he's the Son of God?" Being close to Jesus doesn't automatically make someone a follower. **Mark 3:20-22**

Jesus posed a rhetorical question because he's not seeking an answer. **Matthew 12:50, *"For whoever does the will of my Father in heaven is my brother and sister and mother."*** Instead, he is asking, "Who is my family?" The goal is for you to focus and pay attention. Jesus differentiates between your biological family and your spiritual family. He subtly rebukes his mother and brothers for interrupting him, showing where his priorities lie. When he asks about his mother and brothers being outside, it highlights that, although we have a biological family, the Lord emphasizes the importance of spiritual kinship. Now that you are part of the Kingdom of God, your real family consists of those who follow the will of the Father.

Now that you are part of the Kingdom of God, your true family includes those who follow the will of the Father. Jesus also said in **Matthew 10:34**, *"Do not suppose that I have come to bring peace to the earth. I did not come to bring peace, but a sword."* This sword of division divides those who support Jesus from those who oppose Him, even among your family members with your last name.

There exists a different kind of blood that's far stronger than biological blood. Your spiritual family—your brothers and sisters—is a more authentic family than your unconverted biological relatives. Christ elevates the spiritual family of believers above their earthly families. You are part of this family, with a spiritual lineage that connects back to the cross of Christ. A disciple is someone who learns from Jesus, follows His will, and cares for His people.

When Jesus states, *"Love covers a multitude of sins,"* he emphasizes the importance of supporting each other by carrying burdens, restoring one another, and praying collectively. You may believe you are doing your best, but God's complete plans for you might be beyond your current understanding. These blessings are rooted in your covenant relationships, including your sisters, mothers, and fathers in faith. As a spiritual church family, we come together to share meals, open our homes, and provide financial support. This unity stems from sharing everything in common and holding each other accountable.

We pray for one another. If a family member departs, I will find and bring them back, as we are connected by blood. Through Christ's death, burial, and resurrection, we are given strength to remain united. We are called to share this glorious gospel and stand firm in our faith in Jesus Christ's resurrection until we part from this world as spiritual siblings.

CHAPTER 16

PRAYER

Dear Lord, we humbly acknowledge your glory; all we can do is thank you. Please capture the attention of your sons, daughters, and even those who do not believe. I pray that your kingdom expands. Grant us understanding and stir our hearts. Help us rely on your word and increase our love for the scriptures, freeing us from the desire for human approval, clever words, and man-made doctrines. Strengthen our passion for knowing your word. During these last days, amidst a famine for the word, make us lovers of your holy scriptures and teachings. In your precious name, Lord and Savior, Jesus Christ. Amen.

CHAPTER 17

PARABLES

When God is on your side, failure is impossible. Even if it seems like He's not acting, His success is certain. Whether He responds to your prayers or remains silent on the mountaintop or in the valleys, failure is not an option for Him. He will never let you down, whether He speaks or stays silent on your journey, in any circumstance. Despite my mistakes and failures, I have two choices: I can let them become burdens that weigh me down or use them as lessons to grow, transforming setbacks into valuable learning experiences.

We are involved in a spiritual conflict. Demons are present on Earth, affecting psychics, fortune-tellers, horoscopes, deception, and unstable relationships. People acting unpredictably in public may not be fully accountable; demons often possess them. For some, it's not just substance abuse like heroin—others talk to themselves, influenced by these spirits. They observe prisoners of war. Stay alert! Additionally, Scripture mentions another Kingdom that prophets have predicted for thousands of years. A new kingdom is emerging, starting as a small seed in Israel and growing into a mighty oak. This kingdom will challenge darkness and penetrate people's hearts, ultimately conquering that darkness.

Revelation suggests that when the second Kingdom takes dominance in this battle, the lion will lie down with the lamb. Earthly realms will transform into domains of our gods, and God will live among humans. At present, a cosmic struggle is happening in the spiritual realm around you. This is why some of your thoughts might be harmful and not truly yours. On the other hand, some thoughts come from the Holy Spirit, urging you to ignore negative ones. Because of the ongoing clash between the second and first Kingdoms, many might not realize that Christianity is not only a journey of righteousness and peace but also a form of spiritual warfare.

Understanding this is crucial for truly grasping Christianity. Believing that simply attending church and ignoring the spiritual darkness that seeks to destroy your marriage, children, or attack your mind and heart will guarantee your salvation is a misconception. Even if everything appears perfect externally, many Christians remain unaware because they neglect reading the Scriptures and fail to recognize the ongoing spiritual warfare. A battle is happening for the hearts and souls of people; stay alert. This shows how prayer, especially intercession—praying for others' salvation—is a form of spiritual warfare. Exorcising demons from individuals is another battlefield, rescuing captives.

Leading souls to Jesus is an act of warfare, opening prison doors through gospel preaching and encouraging captives to accept freedom. Saving souls is therefore a spiritual fight. Additionally, sharing truth on social media during dark times is also a form of warfare. As we promote the Kingdom and the church, we should look for more opportunities to save souls, as these are part of spiritual combat.

Gaining a deeper understanding of the scriptures helps clarify Jesus' teachings. While Jesus' phrase, "Repent, for the Kingdom of Heaven is at hand," might appear as mere words, it signifies the coming of the Kingdom of God. His incarnation in the first century AD showcased the power of this Kingdom on Earth. Jesus started sharing this message during John the Baptist's time, as reflected in the saying, "The Kingdom of Heaven suffered violence, and the violent take it by warfare." Many of us overlook the fact that our perception of Jesus' ministry is often narrow, viewing his healings simply as acts of kindness. However, these miracles were more than mere compassion—they were acts of spiritual warfare from an Old Testament viewpoint, demonstrating to Israel that he was conquering darkness through divine power.

Through His miracles, Jesus showed Israel that the Kingdom of God has fully arrived and is more powerful than darkness. While Satan kept people captive, Jesus set them free—not just out of compassion, but to fulfill biblical prophecy; a greater power, the Kingdom of heaven, had entered the world through Jesus. Each time He cast out a demon or welcomed someone into the Kingdom, He was fighting a spiritual battle. This healing went beyond kindness; for instance, He visited the pool of Bethesda, passing sick individuals to heal a man who had been suffering there for 38 years. He also healed a man born blind, and when his sight was restored, witnesses said, "We had never seen anything like this before in history,' affirming that the Kingdom of heaven had arrived. That's why His first sermon started with **"Repent, for the Kingdom of heaven is at hand."** In Christ, the full power of the Kingdom of heaven began ruling on earth.

Since the days of John the Baptist and Jesus, the Kingdom of Heaven has been steadily expanding in all directions. It is spiritually liberating captives and capturing people's hearts and minds until God has gathered everyone meant to belong to Him, right up until we all pass away and join in the marriage feast of the Lamb. Everyone who is saved has been taken out of the Kingdom of Darkness. The Bible makes it clear that you have entered the Kingdom of Light. You transition from death to life, from darkness to light, from blindness to sight. In the 1st century AD, Jesus Christ revealed a set of hidden teachings about how the Kingdom of Heaven functions, its purpose, and its power, all conveyed through parables. Jesus was not the first to teach with parables; Solomon used them in Proverbs, sharing stories with deeper meanings. Others also employed parables in their teachings. However, what set Jesus apart was that, especially in the latter half of his ministry, he taught exclusively through parables.

Jesus shifted from delivering straightforward teachings, like the Sermon on the Mount, to speaking exclusively through parables. In **Matthew 13:34-35,** it says that Jesus shared all these teachings in parables and did not speak to them without one, fulfilling what was spoken through the prophet: **'I will open my mouth in parables; I will declare things kept secret from the foundation of the world.'** From that point on, Jesus's ministry changed. He stopped openly teaching clear doctrines and truths that everyone could understand, opting instead to communicate only in parables. It was as if he declared, "I'm done with direct speech; from now on, I will speak only in parables."

In the gospel attributed to him, **Mark 4:13** states that Jesus mentioned those who do not grasp the parable of the Sower will struggle to understand other parables. This insight is crucial because it serves as a gateway to understanding additional teachings and helps unlock a wider understanding.

Matthew 13:10 questions why Jesus speaks in parables. The disciples then ask Him, giving us this explanation. Curiosity can bring wisdom, yet many miss chances by not asking the right questions to the right people. Seeking advice from older, wiser, and experienced individuals is key to gaining knowledge. Still, some are too proud to ask for help, often struggling alone because pride and fear hold them back. A foolish person depends only on their own experiences, while a wise person learns from others' successes, failures, and experiences.

Don't hesitate to ask God questions.

During my walk with the Lord, I've faced this challenge. I hold deep reverence for God, so I seldom doubt His decisions. When things happen, you may feel like asking Him questions, but remember, He can perceive your thoughts. Your silent ideas aren't secret from

Him; they hold just as much significance as spoken words. The Lord welcomes your curiosity. Even if He doesn't always respond, He isn't deterred by your questions.

It's okay to ask the Lord questions.

Jesus replied when asked about speaking in parables to His disciples, **Matthew 13:11**, "Because the secrets of the kingdom of heaven have been given for you to know, but it has not been given to them."

The first two terms, "reveal" and "conceal," relate to showing and hiding. Jesus primarily uses parables to encode profound truths about the Kingdom of God, which he then shares with his followers through simple stories called parables. These narratives communicate key theological insights about the Kingdom you currently live in and the one where you will ultimately find glory, embedding these truths within stories. To his followers, he reveals the secret Greek word "Mysterion"—the mysteries of the Kingdom. As a result, he teaches through parables and offers explanations to uncover truths about the Kingdom. The parables can be obscure; only those who are saved, familiar with Scripture, and have capable Bible teachers will understand the mysteries of the Kingdom. Each parable relates to the gospel of salvation and the Kingdom.

Are you postponing your preparation until next Sunday? That's similar to waiting for tomorrow, as if today isn't the crucial day for salvation. When you sense God stirring in your heart, that's the time to repent. For those who are saved and filled with the Spirit, we have the Scriptures, which encompass all of God's word. Through them, we learn the secrets and mysteries of the heavenly kingdom that are made known to us.

However, another reason for the use of the Parable was concealment. **Proverbs 25:2** in the Old Testament says, *"It is the glory of God to conceal a matter and the glory of kings to investigate a matter."* This indicates that God takes pride in hiding certain truths from specific individuals. Who was outside when Jesus was inside? The unbelievers. He told them, "I will now only speak to them in parables." But why? In **Matthew 12**, the Pharisees and religious leaders dismiss all his teachings and miracles, even claiming, *"All your power comes from the devil."* Notice

Jesus' response: Because they mock his teachings and deny his powers—accusing him of being possessed by the devil—he says that from now on, they will no longer hear straightforward truths. Due to their rejection of him, he will alter his mode of communication with them.

Therefore, the parables are not merely simple stories for understanding; they function as a means of judgment that confounds those who reject the Lord. By turning away from Him, He's saying, *"I will teach in a way that prevents you from ignoring my truth. You will come to value my truth, but I will keep it hidden within these parables. In rejecting me, you become confused, foolish, and lack knowledge of the Kingdom."* The parables act as a judgment for those who reject Jesus Christ, causing unbelievers to read them without understanding. Meanwhile, for those in the Kingdom, the mysteries and secrets have been revealed, but not to others.

Unbelievers often say either, "I don't want to know God," or "I need to understand this God people talk about."

Parables serve to both reveal and reject, functioning as a form of judgment. They can either increase hunger or lead to rejection. **Matthew 13:12** supports this, stating, "For whoever has, more will be given to him, and he will have more than enough; but whoever does not have, even what he has will be taken away from him." The Lord divides people into two groups: those who have, including Christians, followers of Jesus, and disciples, and those who do not. Gaining knowledge of God through studying the Word and learning the parables leads to growth, deeper understanding, wisdom, and divine secrets. This helps you embody wisdom and understand God's matters more deeply. Conversely, those who reject God — the ones who do not have — will lose even what little they possess.

What does this mean? The more your heart hardens, the less you often gain or experience. You might uncover some truths about God, but if your heart remains hardened toward Him, even those small insights will be lost. Moreover, you miss opportunities to use what you have because you haven't embraced the secrets of the Kingdom. **Matthew 13:13**, "This is why I speak to them in parables, because looking they do not see, and hearing they do not listen or understand."

He engages with others while being aware that some may be too closed off to accept the truth. Therefore, it's important to recognize when someone withdraws and to adjust your language accordingly. Sometimes, silence can be meaningful, and other times, just a simple *"bless you"* is enough. This approach helps safeguard you. **Matthew 13:14-17,** "Isaiah's prophecy is fulfilled in them, which say, **'You will listen and listen, but never understand; you will look and look, but never perceive. For this people's heart has grown callous; their ears are hard of hearing, and they have shut their eyes; otherwise they might see with their eyes, and hear with their ears, and understand with their hearts, and turn back —and I would heal them'** "Blessed are your eyes because they do see, and your ears because they do hear. For truly I tell you, many prophets and righteous people longed to see the things you see but didn't see them, to hear the things you hear but didn't hear them."

Jesus also used parables to fulfill prophecy. In **Isaiah 6:8-11,** He said, *"Then I heard the voice of the Lord asking: Who will I send? Who will go for us?" I said: Here I am. Send Me. And he* *replied: Go! Say to these people: Keep listening, but do not understand; keep looking, but do not perceive. Make the minds of these people dull; defend their ears and blind their eyes; otherwise, they might see with their eyes and hear with their ears, understand with their minds, turn back, and be healed." Then I said, "Until when, Lord?" And he replied: Until cities lie in ruins without inhabitants, houses are without people, the land is ruined and desolate."*

Toward the end of **Isaiah 6,** it is mentioned that God will preserve a remnant for Himself, ensuring that some people on Earth will accept and respond to His truth. The Lord proclaimed, **"*Your eyes are blessed and your ears are blessed.*"** The faithful had yearned to witness what you and I are experiencing, yet never had the chance, while we often take it for granted.

We are part of the Kingdom of Heaven. Now that you see and feel what many have long desired, the Lord reminded us that we often forget our spiritual awareness. We recognize that we are saved, filled with the Spirit, and our names are written in glory. As members of this Kingdom, we can access divine secrets in the Bible that only the saved understand. For example, at work, we possess insights that others lack. We are aware of the impending judgment; they are not. We see the ongoing spiritual warfare around us; they remain unaware. While others might see your husband as irrational, you recognize the devil's influence in him. Because your eyes see and your ears hear, you hold a special, encrypted knowledge that most people do not have.

Chapter 18

Prayer

Father, in Jesus' name, I ask you to develop a strong awareness of the Kingdom in your children. Help them understand the reality of spiritual battles and inspire a curiosity to explore its mysteries, secrets, parables, and wisdom, along with Your sacred Scriptures. We pray for the unbelievers. I ask you to save them where they are, guide them to confess their sins, and surrender at your mercy seat. If you are a sinner who has broken God's laws and feels distant from Him, remember that Jesus died to save you from eternal separation. Turn away from your sin, seek God's forgiveness, and approach His mercy seat, saying, "I'm sorry, I surrender." He is calling you. Salvation is available even now. God, fill them with your Spirit, open their eyes to see the mysteries, secrets, wisdom, parables, and teachings of the Kingdom. I pray this in the powerful, glorious name of Jesus Christ. Amen.

CHAPTER 19

YOUR HEART

It deeply saddens me to see that both men and women are estranged from God. Many individuals today struggle with thoughts that stray from God's Word's guidance. How many are dealing with emotions that lack God's direction? I also wonder how many are making important life choices—like selecting a spouse, deciding who to date, choosing a home, picking a career, or contemplating a move—without grounding their decisions in God's wisdom.

Now is the perfect time to embrace the teachings of Christ.

Two kingdoms are at odds: the Kingdom of Darkness, ruled by Satan, the ancient serpent from the garden who tricked Adam and Eve. He brought sin into the world, causing suffering such as war, death, famine, sickness, suicide, depression, and human conflict. Every pain and tear in this broken world stems from Satan. In contrast, another kingdom exists—the Kingdom of Light, representing God's realm at war with the Kingdom of Darkness. Scripture affirms that it will ultimately triumph. Revelation envisions a future where the world's kingdoms become God's kingdoms, with all knees bowing and tongues confessing Jesus as Lord. Ultimately, there will be one Kingdom, one King, one government, and one rule, resulting in the enemy's defeat.

The embodiment of the Lord Jesus Christ fulfilled the Old Testament promise and brought the Kingdom of Heaven, which had been foretold for thousands of years. Christ proclaimed, "Repent, for the Kingdom of Heaven is near," signaling the powerful arrival of this Kingdom on earth. During His ministry, John the Baptist announced the spreading of God's Kingdom into people's hearts across cities, nations, and the world. Throughout history, millions have honored, worshipped, and joyfully celebrated Jesus as their King.

Don't look for sermons that merely comfort or soothe your feelings. Instead, focus on understanding God's word. God did not elevate a preacher's reputation above His own; He considers His word greater than His name. Although a preacher's words are not promised to be eternal in heaven, His word is everlasting. The Bible emphasizes its unbreakable nature. While many people seek entertainment from men, they often neglect to hear God's true message through preaching.

Matthew 13:18, Jesus says, "So listen to the parable of the sower." The word **"listen"** is crucial. Jesus is guiding his disciples to respond to the gospel message. Some of you might feel like yawning or dozing off when the word is spoken. Instead, try to engage fully with your heart, mind, and spirit. A part of you should be thinking, "Lord, I want to understand the word. I am a mature believer eager for the word." Jesus represents the Sower, serving as a metaphor for personally sharing the gospel, whether one-on-one, in small groups, or on a larger scale, from local churches to entire nations.

Everyone who proclaims the word, whether they're preachers or not, will always encounter four distinct reactions whenever the gospel is shared—be it on a podcast, a platform, or across different nations. When the word is spoken, it's like casting seed. In the parable, this seed represents the word of God, which has the power to generate life and bring about change. Planting a seed in soil can significantly transform that environment. The seed can land in various places, changing settings, transforming homes, and impacting the earth. It carries unlimited potential to transform everything it touches.

Not all seeds represent God's word. Some are genuine, while others are fake. You might also encounter false seeds. Dishonest preachers often spread messages that are diluted and compromised.

Not every sermon contains the seed of God's Kingdom. Jesus clarified that this seed is the word of the Kingdom — not human words, Google's data, or articles; it specifically pertains to the word of the Kingdom. He also explains where this seed is found and how it is planted in the heart. The seed is not placed in the mind but in the innermost part of a person, the heart, which is the source of transformation. Matthew 12:34 states, "For the mouth speaks from the overflow of the heart." That's why someone can know scriptures mentally without a genuine heart transformation. Some quote scriptures as if they are saved, yet their hearts remain unchanged. They might grasp it intellectually, but lack real heartfelt understanding.

Matthew 13:20, "And the one sown on rocky ground- this is one who hears the word and immediately receives it with joy. But he has no root and is short-lived. When distress or persecution comes because of the word, immediately he falls away." This describes a hardened heart. When someone hears the gospel, they often instinctively reject it, showing no desire for a connection with the gospel, Jesus, the Kingdom, or ministry. This includes atheists, agnostics, Muslims, and even the colleague at your workplace or the person you're witnessing to. These individuals react with anger when His name is mentioned or dismiss Him altogether. It can also be a family member who criticizes your efforts with questions like, "Who do you think you are?" These are people who, upon hearing

God's word, immediately tune it out—listening but not truly hearing, as they reject it altogether

When God's word takes root in someone's heart, Satan quickly tries to remove that seed. The dissemination of God's message is often met with spiritual opposition. As the gospel spreads through social media and global platforms, the devil notices when it lands on hard ground and promptly snatches it away. Therefore, we must pray whenever the gospel is preached. We are on the front lines in the struggle to save people from eternal separation from God.

Many of us cherish Jesus as our savior, yet He doesn't have authority over every part of our daily lives. His influence reaches only where we're willing to allow it. When confronted with challenges to our comfort, discomfort with certain truths, or offenses to our beliefs, it reveals areas where we haven't fully surrendered to Him. In these moments, our hearts may become hardened. You encounter a scripture that speaks to you, but then you turn the page.

You hesitate to advocate for unborn children, yet Jesus told Jeremiah, **"I chose you before I formed you in the womb. I set you apart before you were**

born." This may feel overwhelming for you. Your heart has become hardened, blocking the word from reaching you. We must be honest. Even though you love Jesus, there are parts where you do not allow Him full authority. You accept Him only when He doesn't challenge your beliefs. Some people think Jesus only helps them on Sundays, or maybe Wednesdays. As you deepen your relationship with Jesus, you desire conviction over comfort. This shows that His hand stays with you, displaying His love. His conviction exemplifies this love, and His discipline reflects it. **Hebrews 12:6**

Paul spoke to those who recognize their sins in **Romans 1:21-25.** If you ignore repenting due to your desires, the Lord will allow you to pursue them. The greatest danger is when He leaves you to those cravings, but you cannot have both. The most dire state is when you can sin without remorse and still sleep peacefully.

You Need to Be Careful!!

The Parable of the Sower. **Matthew 13:20-21** describes Israel's rocky landscape, which has limestone just below the surface, roughly one to two feet deep.

When planting in this soil, roots proliferate at first but quickly hit the limestone barrier, limiting further growth. The plant may sprout, but under harsh conditions—represented by the sun—as a result, the plant wilts and withers, symbolizing a shallow heart. Some people might feel compelled to hide their Christian faith if it's disapproved of.

A person hears the gospel and begins attending church, engaging with Jesus' teachings. They attend three times a month, might join a team, and occasionally give offerings. They spend time with others, sit in your row, and participate in church activities. Their commitment can last from a week to several years, appearing to be a true believer. We often see them as Christians, calling them our sister or brother, without waiting for clear signs of grace. Eventually, a prophet or false prophet may tell them, **"Turn to Christ; He'll make your life perfect and prosperous, making everything easy,"** leading them to accept Christ based on these promises. Later, they realize, **"In this world, you will encounter tribulation."** When faced with hardships because of their faith, they must decide whether to keep Christianity despite pressure or to abandon it for easier half-measures. Trials reveal who the genuine believers are and who they are not.

Storms reveal who truly supports us and who doesn't. During tough times, watch for those who reach out, stay close, and send prayers. Understand the feelings involved in facing and overcoming hardships; often, sincere friends fade away, and former allies may leave. The scripture indicates that during persecution, some individuals retreat from their faith. The Greek term for 'fall away' suggests taking offense, meaning they become upset by Christianity's demands. People say I love Jesus as long as my spirit remains unchallenged. I love Jesus if everyone approves of me. I love Jesus as long as my lifestyle doesn't disturb others. When faith is easy and comfortable, people feel devoted. But when difficulties arise, they take offense. These people might say, 'I tried Jesus, and it didn't work.'

Some of you need to see God's word not just as a book, but as a source of healing. Reflect on what's happening in your heart and consider what Scripture reveals. Some should go beyond reading for knowledge and begin reading for understanding. You might follow your Bible plan and read chapters, yet still miss true insight. This indicates a preoccupied heart. People hear the gospel, start attending church, and engage actively in their community. They build friendships and work on developing an online Christian ministry. But as their efforts expand, they begin to observe the world, and two influences start to affect them.

The first challenge is worldly cares, where people become preoccupied with life's worries. They get caught up in everyday concerns, which makes them busy and causes them to neglect both gathering and spiritual practices. For instance, they may say, *"I'm building my ministry; I don't have time for the church" or "I don't have time to pray or read."* When you're too busy for God, you are too busy. The pressures of daily life have pushed aside time for scripture, prayer, and community events. Attendings that were once weekly are now every three weeks, then every two, and now only once a month. Many only come for Christmas and Easter. Their hectic schedules leave little room for God. Yet, as Hebrews reminds us, we should not neglect gathering, but rather do so more eagerly as we await Christ's return.

Many believers become frustrated with God for not blessing them with wealth, asking, "Why am I struggling to pay my bills?" God's response is often, "Because I need you to remain in this situation for now." This is because your character might not be strong enough to handle financial blessings; if God granted your requests, it could overwhelm you, like a noose tightening. So, keep working your nine-to-five, face the struggles of bills, and stay involved in community gatherings. When hardships become too much, spend time in prayer. God hasn't said wealth is wrong, but warned about its deceitfulness, which can lead you to trust wealth instead of the giver.

Wealth can be possessed without being dominated by it, but this demands a mature believer with strong faith. Maintaining this balance is achievable as long as Christ remains your highest priority. Some might persist for a while, but eventually, they also fade away. The image of Christ as the sower illustrates the different responses to his message, three of which are false conversions. Jesus is regarded as the most perfect, righteous, and skilled preacher in history; however, despite his teachings, most of his audience rejected his message. The issue isn't with the Sower or the seed (the Bible), but with the people themselves. We all share responsibility, including you. **This should encourage us, as truth-tellers, especially when others oppose us for our honesty.**

Matthew 13:23 "But the one sown on the good ground-this is one who hears and understands the word, who does produce fruit and yields; some a hundred, some sixty, some thirty times what was sown." This individual fears the word itself, listening with their heart and approaching it gently. They seek to understand scriptures and find conviction, wanting truth to challenge them and confront aspects of their life. They long for healing and aim to move beyond brokenness. They no longer wish to entertain negative thoughts and desire the world to remain connected to their mind and heart. Their goal is transformation. They embody the word and understand it on a deep level.

The final type of person is someone with an open heart, passionate about God's teachings. Seeking to understand God's truth to develop conviction and undergo transformation. Welcome challenges and strive to uncover the truth, rejecting falsehoods. People need guidance to recognize their mistakes and support in pursuing righteousness and holiness. Desire God's word to influence their thoughts, feelings, emotions, and choices, impacting all aspects of their life. We should aim to integrate God's word into our marriages, relationships, children, and the lives of those around us.

CHAPTER 20

PRAYER

Heavenly Father, I pray that people around the world keep open hearts, consistently embracing, sharing, understanding, and transforming through God's word. I seek transformation for all hearts that are hardened, rocky, shallow, or distracted—turning them from darkness into light and making them receptive. I pray for all households to encourage conversations between parents and children. May your name be mentioned in everyday moments—whether at the grocery store, laundromat, gym, restaurant, or anywhere else—and may these moments plant seeds of God's word. Amen.

CHAPTER 21

WHERE WILL YOU END UP?

A worldview is a comprehensive perspective on how we see the world. It acts as a lens through which people interpret their experiences, influencing their thoughts and actions. Observing the actions and priorities of the church and Christians in America, along with the issues that concern us and our display of vanity, makes me realize the importance of having a biblical worldview. Many individuals identify as Christians without truly understanding the Bible. Conversely, atheists dismiss the concept of intelligent design, seeing everything as a matter of chance. These perspectives do not align with

God's word, resulting in many people around the world holding flawed worldviews that negatively impact their thoughts and behaviors. As believers, we must strive to develop an evident biblical worldview.

Several key elements shape how we interpret and react to global events. These are essential for maintaining a biblical worldview; without them, our perspective on the world can become distorted. Losing this biblical viewpoint limits our ability to handle modern challenges effectively. The first element is creation. We believe that the perfect life-support system, the order of creation, and the intricate relationship between humans and nature—such as trees producing oxygen and absorbing carbon dioxide—did not happen by chance. When observing the sun and stars, we see intention, not randomness; I have no ancestors that are apes.

God is the creator of everything, including humans and animals. This belief in divine creation, rather than evolution, forms the foundation of a biblical worldview.

The second key aspect of a biblical worldview is the Fall, which teaches that sin entered the world through the enemy's deception, leading humans to rebel against

God. This rebellion resulted in a curse and caused sin to spread worldwide. Recognizing the Fall helps us understand human suffering and see that the brokenness we observe is rooted in it. People without this biblical view might offer different explanations for the world's broken state. But for believers, this perspective enables us to see all forms of societal breakdown, including our own, acknowledging that we are all affected by humanity's original fall. As a result, we interpret the world through the lens of **Genesis 3**.

The third core element of our biblical worldview is redemption. Recognizing current events shows that God's plan for redemption existed even before the fall. As we perform our daily tasks and services, God actively works to redeem people. He is uniting a diverse group from every nation, tribe, and language, with whom He will dwell forever. Although not everyone will be redeemed in this age, God continues gathering His children worldwide. He is assembling a church from all parts of the world for Himself.

The fourth element of a biblical worldview is the concept of consummation, which relates to the end of all things. Scripture reveals that time is finite, showing that God is guiding the world towards its ultimate end and preparing for the conclusion of everything as we understand it. This explains why striving for a perfect utopia on Earth is futile. No ideal society can be created here because, ultimately, flawlessness is unattainable in this world, as God is steering everything toward a divinely destined conclusion. The rapture of the Church is approaching quickly; Jesus' return is closer than many realize. A final moment will come when God concludes everything. This truth is revealed in the Word of God. The only people unaware are those who dismiss His Word.

The last aspect of a biblical worldview is the idea of a new creation, rooted in God's Word. Revelation 20 and 21 show that God will remake the earth, first cleansing it with fire, then restoring it. After this renewal, God will live among His people, with believers dwelling with Him and Jesus ruling forever from Jerusalem. This city will never be destroyed; God protects it because He will return and reign from Jerusalem. This view profoundly shapes how we understand the world.

The story of two kingdoms at war—the Kingdom of Light and the Kingdom of Darkness—highlights the importance of a biblical worldview, God's active influence, our current role, and our priorities. These kingdoms are in perpetual conflict. Jesus came to establish the Kingdom of Light, which continues to grow in people's hearts globally, ultimately overcoming the Kingdom of Darkness and transforming the world's kingdoms into God's Kingdom. He used parables to teach these profound truths about the Kingdom, making them understandable for his followers and serving as a judgment for those who rejected his message.

Matthew 13:24, He presented another parable to them: "The Kingdom of heaven may be compared to a man who sowed good seed in his field." As a follower of Jesus, you live in the Kingdom of heaven. Consequently, everything Jesus taught about this Kingdom is highly significant for you. If you are part of the Lord Jesus Christ, then the parables concerning the Kingdom are essential for your spiritual growth. A farmer planted high-quality seed in his field, while another later spread weeds in the same area.

Farmers plant wheat in their fields, but if they dislike someone, they might secretly sow Darnel weed, a common plant in the Middle East that looks like young wheat. During growth, they are hard to distinguish because of their similar appearance, with the main difference being that Darnel's roots are poisonous. The roots are intertwined, making early identification impossible, and pulling out a weed risks harming a wheat plant. Farmers must wait until harvest to separate them. They instruct laborers to "separate the wheat from the weeds" during collection. The wheat is stored securely, while the weeds are gathered and burned for fuel.

Matthew 13:36 indicated that Jesus' disciples deeply desired his teachings. **Matthew 5:6** states, "Blessed are those who hunger and thirst for righteousness, for they will be filled."

We grow wiser from the Lord by actively seeking His guidance. I encourage you to make it a routine to ask the Lord for direction. Talk to my heart, reveal to me the changes I need to make, and show me what the future holds. Is this person meant to be my husband? Are they genuinely seeking wisdom from the Lord?

As followers of Jesus, we should embrace this principle: cultivate the habit of seeking understanding from the Lord. Frequently, their questions help us learn valuable lessons from the parables, as they sincerely seek God's guidance. They demonstrate a genuine desire for knowledge, a trait we all should nurture for divine insight.

Jesus is the one building the church on earth, taking full responsibility for all the work and deserving all the glory for what happens in our lives. Instead of us doing the sowing, he manages it all himself, since the seed he plants is good. This isn't about morality but about the righteousness of believers, which we receive through Christ's righteousness.

He affirms that the seed he plants is good. Initially, he shares the message and gathers followers, then nurtures them by planting the seed in their hearts. Therefore, those who are saved are saved through the seed of the word. Ultimately, he views you as a seed and sows you. In some regions, the number of believers varies, with certain countries having more followers than others.

Globally, He has sown seeds—millions flourish in some areas, while only a few thousand grow in others. Nonetheless, Jesus gathers His followers, nurtures them with the gospel, and sends them out again. Therefore, everyone who has found salvation has been planted by the Lord Jesus Christ.

It's essential to recognize that the Lord intentionally placed you here. Your unique gifts, talents, abilities, burdens, and concerns are all part of His purpose; this is deliberate, not coincidental. God is aware of this generation's needs and has positioned you in it. No matter where the Lord has placed us, we should stay productive.

Always produce good results wherever you are, until He leads you elsewhere. Remain faithful in your current position. Avoid complaining about your circumstances. Stay committed to where you are because He has a purpose for you. When summoned, you embody salt and light, and He has placed you there to serve that role. Christians are not meant only to go to church.

What is God engaged in? Gathering souls before time expires. The idea of consummation aids in understanding a biblical worldview. We recognize we have been placed here, and now our primary focus should be on advancing God's Kingdom and sharing the gospel. From a biblical perspective, this priority is crucial because we know what lies ahead: judgment and the end of all things.

Your planting is intentional and meaningful. Guided by a biblical worldview, you recognize the significance of this moment and its context. You acknowledge both creation and the fall. With this biblical outlook, you live in redemption during a time when God is actively drawing people to Himself. You are aware of what lies ahead: the consummation and the end. You understand that not everyone will be prepared then. Why would you be an unproductive plant? What purpose does an unfruitful plant serve in this age of redemption? A plant that does not pray, care, or perceive—what significance can it have?

The devil is the one who plants weeds, as Scripture suggests; he sneaks in at night to sow seeds, taking pleasure in causing conflict while staying hidden. Since people are usually unaware during sleep, Scripture highlights the need for alertness. **1Peter:5-8**

Jesus said that He has sown His sons into the world, alongside those sown by the devil. This indicates that on every continent, the sons of God and the sons of the devil coexist, often in the same settings. They are commonly found together in places like rooms, arenas, churches, schools, campuses, or online, living side by side. At times, it can be challenging to tell wheat from weeds. **Reference: 1John 3:10**

The enemy did not pick obvious weeds but instead selected ones that closely resemble the others. As a result, we have the sons of light and the sons of the devil, making it difficult to tell them apart at times. There is evidence for both the saved and the unsaved. Good and evil coexist uneasily in the world, and since we know God did not create them, He cannot be blamed for the evil that exists.

People often misunderstand the question of God's existence and the presence of evil, typically due to a flawed perspective. In contrast, a biblical worldview acknowledges the fallen state of the world and the reality of the devil's children, who were placed here to spread wickedness and harm society. Many who question the causes of school shootings—events that kill innocent children—believe that false religions promoted by deceitful ministers contribute to these tragedies, along with acts such as rape, murder, molestation, and suicide. From a biblical standpoint, these behaviors stem from evil influences. Scripture shows that good and evil coexist, at least temporarily.

The harvest signifies the end of an era. The Lord performs two actions. He recognizes the enemy's presence and reassures His followers that everything will eventually come to an end. Do not assume that moral or good behavior alone guarantees salvation, even among the sons of the devil and your friends and family who are not saved. Some individuals can be very moral yet still be sons of the devil. Others may have attended church their whole lives, yet they remain sons of the devil. Anyone who is not saved, not born again, and does not have the Holy Spirit sealed within them is regarded as a son of the devil. Jesus spoke his own words when he said, "Anyone who is not with me is against me, and anyone who does not gather with me scatters."

When an atheist claims that God's existence is impossible because of global evil, a believer counters by saying that evil originates from a biblical perspective, which considers it a result of the fallen world inhabited by the sons of the evil one. **Matthew 13:40-42,**

"Therefore, just as the weeds are gathered and burned in the fire, so it will be at the end of the age. The Son of Man will send out his angels, and they will gather from his Kingdom all who cause sin and those guilty of lawlessness. They will throw them into the blazing furnace where there will be weeping and gnashing of teeth.

Having a true biblical worldview reveals that a time will come when the Lord splits the heavens and commands His angels, the reapers, to gather those from His Kingdom. The world is rife with sinful actions, and even some self-identified Christians accept sin. The Lord has promised His return and will punish all lawbreakers. Even if you attend church but continue in sin, you might feel secure, but He clearly states that His reapers will ensure no one escapes judgment. This includes corrupt politicians, unrepentant athletes, rappers, false preachers, deceitful prophets, and anyone claiming to be Christian but engaging in sin—such as sexual immorality, lying, stealing, or worshiping anything other than Jesus. He declares, *"I'm coming for all of them."*

For those who think there is no hell, Jesus talked about hell more often than about heaven. He warns that the reapers will collect all the unsaved people you know. As they are taken, they will beg God for forgiveness, but it will be too late. He states, "I'm going to throw them into that fiery furnace, and there will be weeping and grinding of teeth." Great sorrow will occur when they realize they have missed the Kingdom. The grinding of teeth signifies intense pain.

Do you encourage others to share the gospel? Do you pray for missionaries working in neglected areas? Are you pleading with God on behalf of loved ones, asking for their eyes to be opened? When did you last mourn for someone distant from God? Instead of merely attending church as a spectator, take an active role in God's mission. Don't be like unproductive wheat sown without purpose. Get involved in what Jesus is doing.

If we neglect our duties in the field, who will take responsibility? If we fail to pray, who will do it? If we do not support gospel ministry, who will fill that gap? The end times are approaching, but grace is still available to offer people a chance to repent. Envision your life as deeply grounded in the Kingdom. What are you willing to give in return? Total surrender.

Those committed to His glory will be fully redeemed and glorified. Their life's purpose is to honor Him, and in the afterlife, they will receive glory. Yet, we often pursue glory for ourselves now. Our true calling is to bring Him honor, and in return, He will glorify us in the next life, making us shine like the brightest sun. Ultimately, our primary aim should be to be fruitful in this life. **Matthew 13:43,** "Then the Righteous will shine like the sun in their Father's kingdom. Let anyone who has ears listen."

Are these elements part of your prayers? Do they impact your giving? Do they affect your worship? Do they mold your lifestyle? I appreciate how the Father brought the Son from heaven, placed Him on earth, and allowed Him to be broken. He then raised the Son with complete power, enabling Him to spread the gospel, nurture His followers, and establish them on earth so they can raise more men and women who will, in turn, build others.

Our lives are meant to focus on Kingdom work, prayer, and our pursuits. Our failure to fully realize our potential and meet the Father's expectations often stems from a distorted worldview. I hope we prioritize Jesus' teachings over the words of others. When will we take time to listen to what the Lord is saying to us? By attuning ourselves to the Lord's messages, we can strengthen our relationship with Him.

All that's needed is to set aside time for prayer, study the scriptures, and read quietly while reflecting. **Philippians 2:5, *"Adopt the same attitude as that of Christ Jesus."*** Pray and let Jesus' words fill your heart and mind. Over time, you'll start sharing His concerns, thinking like Him, and valuing what He loves. Gradually, you'll come to dislike what He despises.

How can you truly have the mind of Christ if you don't understand His words? John 1:1 states, ***"In the beginning was the word, and the word was with God, and the word was God."*** Take a moment to examine your heart's state and your ongoing desires. Consider what you currently regard as most important. If you have clothing, food, and a secure place to live, you should feel content. Dedicate your life to serving Him.

CHAPTER 22

PRAYER

Heavenly Father, wake us up, your children of the Kingdom. Refresh our hearts with your love. Save us from indulging in sin, secret sins, and false pleasures, trusting we can escape their consequences. Give us pure hearts and lives dedicated to you. Help us ignore the distractions of superficial American preaching and cultivate a sincere love for your Word that we study eagerly. Grant us the strength to remain in your presence and pray consistently. Make us truly attentive as we look at the sky, anticipating your return. Help us mourn our losses, whether of loved ones or those who are far from you. Remind us that time is precious and that harvesters seek the lost. Inspire us to pray and spread the gospel worldwide. Let sharing your Word be our primary purpose. I pray in the powerful name of our Lord and Savior, Jesus Christ. Amen.

CHAPTER 23

THE COST

Throughout history, many people have opposed evil, risking or sacrificing their lives for the faith we hold dear today. Every time you pick up the English Bible, remember those who risked their lives so you could have a copy of God's Word. Think about the Bible you often overlook or neglect—gathering dust, avoided while reading, or left on your car's floorboard. Let this serve as a reminder to honor our brothers in faith who sacrificed everything so that you could possess the Bible.

This is the kind of conviction that God's people should exemplify. They ought to live with this strong faith and be recognized for their commitment to holiness, righteousness, and justice before God. Compromise shows weakness of the flesh and indicates a Christian who is afraid to stand for Jesus Christ. Now, more than ever, God needs His people to rise and defend Him in today's world. Beliefs in righteousness, holiness, character, integrity, and faithfulness to Scripture should be a shared testimony among believers. This demonstrates both your testimony and mine.

We all have a Conscience.

Matthew 14:14. John The Baptist's Death

Herod's family was troubled, driven by a quest for power—marrying relatives and asserting Jewish identity. Herod felt guilt over his lack of faith in Christ. Despite lacking the Spirit, he was troubled by the murder of an innocent man, a reaction similar to that of atheists or those denying God's existence. Everyone is born with a conscience reflecting God's presence— the moral law. This inner sense helps us discern right from wrong, indicating that everyone has a conscience (con-science); 'con' meaning 'with' and 'science' meaning 'knowledge.' God implanted a conscience and awareness of His presence in each person.

This explains why, even in areas where the gospel hasn't reached, people still feel guilt over murder. Feelings of remorse for lying, cheating, or other misdeeds are also widespread. But where does this guilt come from? It originates from the conscience, which is anchored in the moral code God has inscribed on each person's heart.

So, I ask an atheist who says, *"Well, **God doesn't exist.**"* Have you ever felt regret for your actions? Yes. Well, where does that moral sense come from? How can those who deny God's existence feel guilty about murder or other sins? The answer is that God has revealed Himself mainly through the conscience He has given us—a moral compass guiding us to distinguish right from wrong. This points to the existence of a higher authority beyond humanity.

Maturity involves consistently being thankful when you feel conviction about sin. Although some may weep and experience guilt because of these feelings, a more troubling scenario, as Paul pointed out to the church in Rome, is when individuals suppress their conscience to justify their actions. They silence their inner voice, enabling sin to flourish. The most perilous situation is when you feel no conviction at all; that is a condition to avoid. It indicates that God might be permitting you to indulge in sin and idolatry, showing a harmful level of attachment.

I am grateful to stay under God's protection. I appreciate His conviction because it reminds me of His guidance. It's crucial to stay connected to His direction. When you experience conviction and your conscience is alert, it shows your heart remains open to challenges and growth. Feelings of guilt affirm the existence of a creator, support a moral code, and acknowledge an authority beyond humanity.

John the Baptist openly denounced his idolatries, adulteries, and sins, refusing to overlook them. Consequently, he was arrested and imprisoned due to Herodias, the wife of his brother Philip (**Matthew 14:4-5,** since John had been telling him, "It is not lawful for you to have her." Although Herod wanted to kill John, he feared the crowd, as they regarded John as a prophet.

John openly criticized a man acting immorally. Why would he confront a pagan king about morality, especially when this king claimed to be Jewish and said he followed Israel's laws? John observed King Herod engaging in actions that contradicted God's word, and he decided not to stay silent. He refused to ignore the misconduct.

We need to arrive at a point where dismissing sin is no longer acceptable. Righteous anger should originate from acknowledging our sins. We should be troubled by our shortcomings—be it lust, envy, judgment, or criticism. We must cease ignoring our sins and permit ourselves to feel anger about them. As God's people and His image-bearers, we are also tasked with showing righteous indignation toward sins within the church and in the world.

For example, John didn't overlook Herod's sin; he recognized the transgression against God's word. He directly confronted the king, saying, 'What you're doing is not lawful,' which ultimately resulted in his imprisonment. John sets the example we should follow. In such moments, we often hesitate to listen. The scriptures guide us on how to live. He shared crucial truths, and if believers do not start speaking out... If we remain silent in the presence of evil, who will carry the message of truth?

If we overlook ungodliness in our nation, ignore idolatry, or fail to promote holiness, who will take up this responsibility? When guided by the Spirit and the word, and when a moment demands action, we must address hypocrisy within the church. We should oppose compromise and superficial beliefs. This isn't authentic Christianity; it is influenced by American culture. We need to challenge these ideas, and doing so doesn't always require confrontation. Sometimes, simply sharing the truth is enough to encourage someone to stand up for what is right.

I believe God's people have both a moral right and a duty to speak out, uphold the truth, and seek understanding. We represent a single ultimate truth, as Jesus said, "I am the way, the truth, and the life." There is one actual truth, distinct from falsehoods that claim to be truth. If followers of God do not proclaim, demonstrate, and articulate this truth, then who will stand up for truth today? We should not overlook sin; recognizing the right moment to confront it is essential.

Satan is a tempting spirit that manipulates insecurities to divert us from God and guides us toward the idolatry of the Antichrist. His alluring influence can captivate us and draw us to an altar that distances us from God.

Matthew describes John during his roughly one-year imprisonment under Herod. What events occurred during John's confinement before his execution? **Matthew 11:2-3,** *Now when John heard in prison what the Christ was doing, he sent a message through his disciples and asked him, "Are you the one who is to come, or should we expect someone else?"*

Consider this: John the Baptist, who was raised alongside Jesus, recognized Him as the Son of God. He preached to the crowds, calling Jesus the Lamb that takes away the world's sins. When baptizing his cousin, he said, *"I must decrease so He can increase."* Yet, while in prison and feeling discouraged, he began to doubt Christ's true identity. John felt disillusioned due to his false expectations of God, believing that the Lord would set up a military kingdom to overthrow Rome and free him. Jesus then explained, "John, you need to decrease while I must increase; your work ends when mine begins."

However, our reactions often mirror each other during tough times. When God doesn't answer as we hope—when opportunities are blocked, relationships break down, marriages end, prayers go unanswered, loved ones pass away, or our deepest hopes are unmet—we become restless due to our unrealistic expectations of God. These unmet expectations can foster feelings of anger towards Him. At times, we might feel our prayers go unanswered, leading to discouragement, disillusionment, or the belief that God isn't listening.

Matthew 11:4, Jesus replied to them, "Go and report to John what you hear and see: The blind received this sight, the lame walk, those with leprosy are cleansed, the deaf hear, the dead are raised, and the poor are told the good news, and blessed is the one who isn't offended by me."

Jesus references the prophet Isaiah to comfort John, highlighting Isaiah's message: "You see the things I do; that proves I am the Messiah. I am the one you spoke about, John." This is more than just reassurance; it serves as a heartfelt reminder through Scripture. When your heart and soul are wounded, God's Word can bring comfort. Some find false reassurance in misleading sermons and wrong teachings, which build unrealistic expectations of God. Although Jesus promised that you would encounter tribulations in this life, some believe they are protected from hardships.

John 16:33, "I have told you these things so that in me you may have peace. You will have suffering in this world. Be courageous! I have conquered the world." You think everyone will appreciate you, but Jesus warned, **John 15:18,** "If the world hates you, understand that it hated me before it hated you."

The word of God isn't just empty words or deceptive teachings. Jesus comforted John in his suffering through God's word, without promising immediate relief, which is clear since Herod eventually executed John. Even when God's plan doesn't involve changing the situation, He still assures us, *'I will transform you from within through the word I give.'*

Sometimes, prayer may not change circumstances, but it can bring peace. When you're in pain, others should understand that comforting phrases like 'You'll get out of this' may not provide absolute comfort. David observed that his suffering served a purpose, helping him to grasp God's ways. **Isaiah 55:8, *"For my thoughts are not your thoughts, and your ways are not my ways."***

To understand and resolve your heart's confusion, expectations, and pain, immerse yourself in God's word. This process involves transforming your character by embracing His Word.

Herod never intended to kill John, but his desire to please others compelled him to do so. Occasionally, our urge to satisfy others leads to poor choices. Trying to please everyone can restrict our independence. We should be confident in saying, "Thus says the Lord," even if it offends. Many of God's followers struggle to stand for the truth because they prioritize pleasing others over remaining steadfast.

The gospel remains unstoppable. As the end of the church age nears, our time as a community is limited. Do you see how the devil is flooding society with heresies, false doctrines, deception, and disrespect for God? If God's people—His sons and daughters—don't proclaim His message, who will defend the truth? If we don't speak out, preach, and stand for righteousness, who will do so in society? The truth often comes at a high cost. Standing up for what is right may cost you friends and hurt your reputation in certain social circles. Some might even refuse to invite you to preach or speak, limiting your influence. Still, I value losing human approval far less than losing God's.

As followers, we must always stand for the truth in every situation—whether on campuses, in schools, in workplaces, in gyms, or on social media. I pray the Lord fills you with righteous anger and a holy indignation against all wickedness, evil, sin, and ungodliness. I urge you to despise sin, turn away from idolatry, and oppose mocking Jesus. Do not fear standing up for the truth. If we neglect to share the Word, lift Christ, teach sound doctrine, and confront false prophets, the devil will take control of our nation.

You've heard the saying: "Evil flourishes when good people do nothing." Christ came, lived perfectly, died sacrificially, was resurrected in power, and bore witness to that truth. We are called to pursue Him. What impact can He have without our testimony or demonstration of faith? Is Jesus just a few hours on a

Sunday? That appears superficial and inadequate. Is that the full extent of Christianity?

CHAPTER 24

PRAYER

Father God, we come before you, asking for your extraordinary strength so we can immerse ourselves in your eternal Word—the only truth rooted in heaven. Please grant us understanding and insight. Lord, reveal any hidden truths and bring them to our awareness. I ask that you remove any unseen chains and heavy burdens, laying them at your feet. Let them remain there through your words and promises. Whisper to us. Replace hardened hearts with hearts of flesh. Tear down pride and arrogance. Remove the blinders from our eyes. Move us beyond cultural Christianity. Please give us the spiritual stamina to sit in your presence. May we hear your heart crying out and live in obedience to you. May we hate what you hate and love what you love. We glorify your mighty name, Lord and Savior, Jesus Christ. Amen.

CHAPTER 25

CARING FOR OTHERS

If you understand scripture, you can discern who genuinely belongs to God and who is guided by the devil. Therefore, it's crucial to recognize a person's character and judge them based on their actions. Shouldn't God's followers show compassion for brothers and sisters impacted by false teachings? Should they feel empathy for people without homes, those who are hungry, and those who are in need? Should they care for men and women trapped in depravity, without hope except through the Holy Spirit and Christ's regeneration? Shouldn't we extend compassion to those around the world who have never heard the gospel and face the risk of dying in their sins? This truly reflects the heart of Jesus.

Matthew 14:14, *When he (Jesus) went ashore, he saw a large crowd, had compassion on them, and healed their sick.*

The Greek word for compassion emphasizes a profound emotional connection rooted in genuine empathy for others. When Jesus sees the people on the shore, he initially considers his own needs but quickly shifts his attention to helping others. This reminds me of times when we face personal challenges. When someone contacts us in distress, and we try to support them, we often hide our tears. As we listen to their struggles and pray silently, ***"God, give me the strength and wisdom to support my brother or sister despite my pain,"*** we are preaching, all while we're experiencing our suffering. In such moments, it's vital to remain focused on supporting others, even as we deal with our hardships.

I know how intense pain can be, whether from depression, grief, or illness. In such times, I often put others' needs before my own, shifting my focus from my struggles to theirs. This approach helps me cope with my pain by concentrating on the greater challenges faced by others. Sometimes, pain is an inherent part of our ministry journey. I continue serving despite suffering, facing challenges, and overcoming difficulties. Even with inner turmoil, I remain dedicated to sharing the truth.

A key aspect of the Lord's character is His ability to adapt effectively. Why does He show compassion? When He sees a large crowd, He looks beyond faces; He recognizes individuals who need salvation. He notices the sickness and those in need of healing. He also perceives people influenced by the false teachings of the Pharisees and Sadducees, who enforce heavy, man-made rules instead of guiding others with God's true principles. He observes those who are exhausted and identifies those who are feeling anxious. He understands who needs help. Although it can be challenging to show compassion now, I want to keep encouraging everyone: the Lord sees everything. Remember these three truths: the Lord sees, the Lord knows, the Lord cares.

Seeing the suffering people on the shore, he was deeply moved with compassion. His heart went out to those trapped by false teachings, those facing physical hardships, and individuals in moral despair seeking salvation. His reaction to all of them was one of compassion. We should feel compassion for people with misguided beliefs. Those who lack clothing, food, and shelter deserve our kindness. It's important to keep praying for those who are away from God. We must not overlook their suffering; instead, let our hearts be filled with compassion for them.

Matthew 14:15, When evening came, the disciples approached him and said, "This place is deserted, and it is already late. Send the crowds away so that they can go into the villages and buy food for themselves." "They don't need to go away," Jesus told them. "You give them something to eat."

Initially, He was not driven by their physical hunger or needs. When the Lord saw a people in distress, His first response was to teach them. He valued imparting God's word more than monetary help or outreach efforts. After all, giving clothing to a homeless person is pointless if they are unaware of the gospel and headed toward hell. Similarly, outreach is ineffective if it doesn't include sharing the gospel. The Lord considered teaching a vital act of compassion.

In America, we often expect to share God's word in a quick 60-minute session—engaging with Jesus briefly before moving on. After six days immersed in secular life, it becomes difficult to focus on more profound teachings. Busy schedules across the country lead us to believe we can sense God's presence in just 20 minutes, hoping to see His movement in that short time. This mindset explains why revivals are rare; we tend to limit God's work to our small time frames instead of giving Him space to operate fully in our lives. You might ask why your mind and heart still feel uneasy and doubt your faith's strength. Many struggle to spend quality time with God through prayer, studying His Word, or sitting quietly to listen.

There appears to be a shortage of spiritual endurance among Americans. Believing that a short 5-minute devotion can significantly change your life is a misunderstanding; expecting profound transformation from only five minutes of prayer each day is unrealistic.

Many churches organize approximately 35-minute services, designed to be concise and boost attendance in subsequent weeks. How long has this tradition lasted? I pray that someday, America experiences enough persecution that people genuinely appreciate coming together in church with fellow believers. May God shake the very foundation of our nation and free us from complacency and apathy, inspiring us to gather in His presence eagerly. Our primary goal should be to be with Him.

Notably, in the text, the disciples didn't ask Jesus, ***"What should we do about the people's needs?"*** Instead, they act independently when they suggest sending the people away. Before criticizing them, consider whether you might respond similarly in challenging situations. We often follow this pattern: in times of difficulty, we tend to ignore seeking God's guidance and instead rely on our judgment. This behavior resembles Eve's temptation with the tree, symbolizing a desire to elevate ourselves to God's level. As a result, we try to control our lives.

During tough times, our first instinct isn't to seek the Lord's advice but to depend on our perceptions and act on them. In difficult times, seek out the one who is the author and finisher of your faith. Turn to the one full of wisdom and knowledge. Follow the one who has already charted the way, as stated in **Isaiah 55:6,** *Seek the Lord while He may be found; call to Him while He is near.*

Matthew 14:16, "They don't need to go away," Jesus told them. "You give them something to eat." He was urging them to take responsibility, since they hadn't asked him for help.

I often think about how we frequently face challenges, which could be tests from the Lord to see how we respond. He shows that He permits these situations to occur. We should be alert in seeking His guidance, studying the scriptures, and avoiding trying to handle everything ourselves. The Lord always has a solution for us, but we often lack the humility to seek it.

The Lord surrounds you with His name and Spirit, blessing you in return. He humbles you on your sanctification journey and then grants you the strength to serve others. If you're experiencing a breaking process, hold on. Often, breaking precedes blessing and service. Before receiving, your will must be broken, idols taken down, and perversion shattered. Developing self-reliance is essential before you can walk confidently. This breaking process should be ongoing as you receive divine blessings. Some might say that God is the one doing the breaking, and they may be right.

Sometimes, out of His kindness, the Lord involves you in your miracle, ensuring that while He is working externally for you, He also strengthens your faith from within as He guides you through this journey. In all circumstances, my God remains in control. Nothing is too complicated for Him or for us when we follow His will, which He governs.

What is the meaning behind the miracle 'Feeding of the Five Thousand'? In

John 6:35, "I am the bread of Life." Jesus was teaching the people that He is the Bread of Life.

He communicates with people, emphasizing that while some seek physical healing, his core message is that he is their true need. I, Jesus Christ, am all they require— more than material possessions. I am the bread of life sent from heaven. This miracle highlights our urgent need for Jesus. In our independence, we pursue temporary pleasures, but your heart is currently filled with stale, false bread. You believe happiness comes from wealth, perfect homes, or ideal spouses, thinking these will fulfill and complete you. Only Lord Jesus Christ, the Son of God who ascended from glory, can satisfy the deep longing in your heart that nothing or no one else can fulfill.

Isaiah 55:3 *Pay attention and come to me; listen, so that you will live. I will make a permanent covenant with you on the basis of the faithful kindness of David.*

Those without resources cannot buy salvation or righteousness, nor can they afford this divine invitation. God issues it: come to me, and I will meet your needs. Offer yourself completely, and I will give you fulfillment. Why spend your money on things that do not truly nourish? The Lord shows that our pursuits and desires do not lead to absolute satisfaction. Do you believe that obtaining these things will truly fulfill your heart? He reminds us that these pursuits are just illusions.

The actual source that can fulfill your deepest soul desires to establish a personal, close relationship with Jesus. This connection involves prayer, studying His Word, confessing sins, resting in His presence, worshiping, crying, and delving into scripture. Love Jesus wholeheartedly, prioritizing Him above all else. Elevate Him in your life, crave Him more than anything, and pursue Him sincerely. He surpasses everything, is present everywhere, and is the genuine longing of your heart. Truly, He is your daily bread.

This passage emphasizes the core of Christology: seeing Jesus as the bread of life, not just pursuing worldly things. People often chase shallow knowledge, but what truly matters is recognizing our need for Christ, beyond just claiming salvation. I long for a sincere relationship with Him. In essence, do you believe the Lord speaks this way from His heavenly throne? No, He fervently proclaims, ***"You give them something to eat!"*** His appeal to His church, His body, and His bride is driven by compassion. Whenever we encounter those far from God—homeless, suffering, or oppressed by injustice and false religion—we are called to respond with compassion.

Instead of just blaming politicians for global issues or waiting for our Commander in Chief to resolve everything, remember that the true answer lies in the gospel and Christ. Let us witness Christ daily and nurture compassion for a troubled world. We are called to be Christ's representatives, shining lights in darkness. "Give them something to eat"—allow compassion to fill your heart. Your mission is to care for the hungry by feeding, clothing, praying, sharing the truth, spreading the gospel, and staying steadfast. Don't wait; be ready to testify.

CHAPTER 26

PRAYER

Dear Lord, I ask for an awakening now. Remove our complacency, for this truly matters. Baptize us with holy compassion and fire. Open our blinded eyes to see the brokenness around us, trapped in poverty, facing urgent physical needs, or suffering under false teachings. Father, I pray that you instill in us the love described in 1 John 3:16, so we won't overlook those in need. I ask for revival within this church, so we may love what you love and hate what you hate. Please make us your eyes, voice, hands, and feet to recognize society's brokenness and human suffering.

CHAPTER 27

THE STORM

The Sea of Galilee is a historic and magnificent body of water, known as the place, where Lord Jesus Christ called his first followers: Peter, James, Andrew, and John. On the southern shore lies the city of Magdala, where an unexpected follower of Jesus, a woman named Mary—whom Christ expelled seven demons— became one of the first to witness the resurrected Christ on that glorious Sunday morning. It was here that Jesus's ministry began to grow and prosper. The Sea of Galilee is also where Jesus performed the miracle of feeding five thousand men, excluding women and children. This extraordinary miracle of food multiplication happened on its shores, the exact location where Jesus restored Peter, a man who had stumbled.

Jesus embodies restoration, and a remarkable miracle occurred in the Sea of Galilee during the 1st century A.D. This event, along with others in scripture, provides a theological foundation for understanding the complex relationship between God's perfect will and life's storms. A key incident in the Sea of Galilee during that time offers us valuable insight into this often complex relationship, especially for those of us in America. It highlights the connection between God's perfect will and the adversities, trials, and challenges He allows within His divine plan.

Feeding the Five Thousand.

John 6:14-15

When the crowd saw the multiplying of loaves and fish, they thought, "This must be the prophet; let's plan a coup. We should overthrow the Roman authorities and declare Jesus king immediately." Sensing their intention to crown him, Jesus escaped to avoid becoming king. He knows He is the King and that His crowning will happen eventually, but He understands that the right time has not yet arrived. He observes that people are acting based on their fleshly desires, as they have been conditioned to do. They are attempting to elevate Jesus to kingship, but the Lord understands that this is not His designated platform. You are trying to make me king without fulfilling my Father's will.

Learning about Jesus has revealed to me how essential discernment is for identifying platforms that truly align with God's will and recognizing when we might be projecting our own desires. This is particularly relevant today, in a culture driven by relentless ambition. People pursue platforms, stages, microphones, and validation, frequently attempting to build monuments that emphasize themselves. However, God understood that their praise for Him was not in line with His true purpose. The kingship they anticipated for Jesus conflicted with His plans, as they acted according to their wishes. If Jesus had doubted Himself, He might have said, 'Go ahead and crown me then.'

The Lord, trusting in His judgment, recognized that this was not the Father's will. We need to develop discernment to distinguish what to avoid outside God's plan. Just because something looks good doesn't mean it's meant for us by God. An open door doesn't necessarily mean it's God's direction. Not all open doors are from God, and not every handshake or chance is divinely appointed. Therefore, we must exercise discernment to know when to hold back, as some opportunities may lie outside God's plan. That's why it's essential to be led by the Spirit rather than driven by our flesh or insecurities.

Some of us are so eager to pursue everything except Christ that we hastily seize opportunities. We often forget to pause and reflect that, even if something appears good and virtuous, it may not align with God's will. A wise and mature individual can turn down something that looks promising, grand, or glorious, understanding that an open door doesn't automatically indicate it's God's plan for their life.

The Lord does not permit His followers to remain on the shore, unlike those enslaved by fleshly desires. Instead, He instructs them to enter a boat, distancing them from the crowd—those at risk of drifting away from God's will. **Matthew 14:22**

The Lord's guidance applies to you and me right now. How many times has God's word tried to steer you away from actions outside His will? How often has the Holy Spirit wanted to guide you away from things that oppose God's desires? Reading the New Testament makes it clear that God's word, the Lord's voice, urges us to turn from behaviors that contradict His will. The Lord seeks to guide you away from immorality, sexual sin, deceit, false prophets, mental strongholds, negative influences, gossip, slander, and sexual relationships outside marriage.

In the New Testament, you'll hear the Lord's voice guiding you away from paths outside His will. You'll feel the Spirit convicting you when facing situations that oppose God's plan. Even if you resist this conviction, engage in superficial ministry, or seek ego flattery, deep down, you will resent the feeling of conviction. As you age, you'll observe the profound love the Lord holds for you. He'll steer your heart clear of anything that strays from God's plan for your life.

After a day of feeding, healing, and preaching, He first seeks God's presence. He seeks sacred silence, reflecting the natural cycle of work and quiet contemplation. The Lord shows us that hard work should be balanced with sacred solitude, where effort is paired with prayer in the secret place. Embracing a hustle-focused mindset, staying endlessly busy, and neglecting time with God isn't truly virtuous. **Matthew 14:23,** *After dismissing the crowds, he went up on the mountain by himself to pray.* Well into the night, he was there alone.

If we are too busy to seek God's presence, we are neglecting what truly matters. We deceive ourselves into thinking we are in control, acting as gods of our own lives, and believe we can perform God's work for a long time without renewal from the Father's presence. We need to find a balanced way to serve the Lord while staying closely connected to Him. Many wrongly assume that their ministry is directly linked to their relationship with Christ, believing that active service guarantees a strong bond. Faithful ministry should stem from a deep personal relationship with Jesus. He models a pattern of work and renewal, characterized in Scripture as an ongoing exchange of prayer filled with power, grace, and guidance. The Lord gives continually and remains ever-renewed.

How much more do we need to seek the Father's presence? Many of you feel burnt out, exhausted, and frustrated because of a lack of prayer in your lives. Some are trying to handle everything by themselves. How has that approach worked for you? Sometimes, a brief prayer is all we can give, and that's perfectly fine. As followers of Jesus, it's crucial to spend time in God's presence regularly. Some might hesitate to approach God, believing they can't stay longer than five minutes. However, I've found that it's in that quiet moment that God often does His deepest work in us. Cultivating the habit of being with God is essential.

Nothing is more vital than being in the presence of Almighty God. When you're near Him, God works most powerfully within you. This is the place where you can honestly admit your sins and shortcomings. In His presence, He reveals where we've gone astray and offers guidance. He also gives warnings in this space, and it is here that He transforms our hearts. Additionally, in His presence, He reveals Himself to us on a deeper level.

God will shape His deepest work within your mind and heart when you intentionally spend time in His presence. Take a walk, listen to worship music, find a quiet space at home, or have some solitary time in a room. Set aside specific moments each week to connect with the Lord—detaching from your spouse, children, ministry, and work. Sit quietly with Him, pray, read the Bible, and ask God to reveal Himself: "Lord, show me myself in Your presence." As you develop spiritually, you'll realize that sometimes, just being close to Him is enough.

Trusting The Lord In The Storm.

Twelve men in a small boat battled crashing waves as the wind howled loudly. While Matthew doesn't go into detail, it suggests they sailed directly into a storm. At first, the weather was calm, but now they are caught in a raging tempest. The quiet aspects of this storm reflect the real challenges we face in life. **Matthew 14:24,** *Meanwhile, the boat was already some distance from land, battered by the waves, because the wind was against them.*

Did Christ realize the path He was guiding them on when they left the seashore? Was He aware of how much they would develop before encountering trials? Did He foresee they would face a storm right after

175

being sent out? Matthew explained that Jesus told them to get into a boat and sail to the other side. This was not merely a suggestion or their own idea; the Lord was aware they would encounter a storm, and it probably was part of His plan for them to go through it.

The pattern is similar in both my life and yours. Some people recognize what it means to have a time of peace—living according to God's will, obeying Jesus, and adhering to their faith. Suddenly, challenges arise—trauma, conflicts, tests, and even demonic attacks—even when we're still within God's plan. Not all trauma is caused by the devil, nor is every difficulty Satan's work. Some struggles might seem like Satan's doing, but ultimately, God allows these hardships. You've stayed faithful to Christ and followed His path, but relationships may falter or betrayals may happen. Many of us can relate to doing everything God asks, yet still facing unexpected hardships we never thought would come.

Some of us encounter difficulties, but this isn't due to any fault or lack of God's love. Instead, God intentionally guides us into these storms. Just as the Spirit led Jesus into the wilderness for temptation, we also experience traumas, hardships, and trials. Some situations you and I face aren't meant for us; the Lord permits us to go through these challenges and difficulties.

The ship was battered by the waves, showing they were rowing against resistance. The text does not mention any attempt to turn back. They kept going for hours in one direction despite the difficulties, with no sign of trying to change course. From this, I understood that when you're aligned with God's will, you can trust that you're making the right choice. Even if challenges occur because of that decision, you should not let them prevent you from persevering.

Many of us face temptation when we commit to a path. You start a journey inspired by divine calling, and suddenly, challenges appear. The temptation is strong; spiritual battles seem fierce, storms unyielding, and when things don't go as planned, you may consider retreating. But retreat to what?

Are you contemplating a return to your old ways? Will you go back to the church you were advised to leave? Are you rethinking the job He told you to quit? Are you reconnecting with the relationship He instructed you to leave behind? Remember, what you left behind was just a season you've outgrown, and in God's Kingdom, moving forward is the only way. Facing challenges while pursuing God's will doesn't mean you should revert to your past; keep progressing, even when trials appear.

In Matthew 14:25, Jesus approaches them walking on the sea early in the morning. This is extraordinary because no one else has done this before. Jesus walking on water is unique; Muhammad did not walk on water or perform miracles, nor did Joseph Smith. No religious founder has ever walked on water. Jesus could have taken a boat or gone around the Sea of Galilee, but instead, he walked on the water to reach them. The Old Testament, well before Christ's time, describes God's unseen footprints as he parts the sea in **Psalm 77:19,** saying, *"Your way went through the sea in your path through the vast water, but your footprints were unseen."*

The disciples had traveled almost across the entire sea, facing hardships, and the Lord waited until they were nearly at the shore to meet them. This message is for everyone who has thought, "Lord, I've been in this situation for a long time. I've been handling these challenges for a long time. I've been enduring this conflict for a long time. I've been fighting this issue for a long time."

He depicts a God who walks on water without leaving any trace. Centuries afterward, Jesus intentionally sends His disciples into a storm and walks toward them on the water, fulfilling scripture and revealing Himself to these twelve men. His walk on water embodies the Word made flesh. The figure I call Lord and Savior is animating the ancient scriptures, representing the fulfillment of the Old Testament; He is the Word made flesh. **John 1, *"In the beginning was the Word, and the Word was with God, and the Word was God."* John 1:14, *The Word became FLESH and dwelt among us. We observed his glory, the glory as the one and only Son from the Father, full of grace and truth.***

Matthew 14:26-27, *When the disciples saw him walking on the sea, they were terrified. "It's a ghost!" they said, and they cried out in fear. Immediately Jesus spoke to them.* "Have courage! It is I. Don't be afraid." The Lord does not criticize them for feeling scared in this passage. A common mistake in America is to make people feel guilty about experiencing fear. Fear is a natural human response to circumstances beyond our control or change; anyone in such a situation would probably feel afraid.

I want you to see the wisdom of the Lord and the grace He shows in their fear. He offers comfort through His Word and presence, which extend to us as well. During times of anxiety, fear, depression, loneliness, or sadness, remember that His Word and presence can bring reassurance. Seeking comfort in the Psalms and Proverbs, and finding peace in both the Old and New Testaments.

While we often seek comfort from various vices, genuine solace is found in God's word and His presence. Many, including myself, carry the heavy weight of trauma. Spending time with God—whether through a walk, listening to worship music, or quiet moments—can significantly reduce anxiety. In His presence, feelings of fear, worry, and anxiety diminish. Next time you need comfort, turn to God's word and seek His presence. Read the scriptures, just as He comforted the disciples with His words and presence. He will do the same for you.

Matthew 14:28-29, *"Lord, if it's you,"* **Peter answered him, *"command me to come to you on the water."* He said,** "Come." **And climbing out of the boat, Peter started walking on the water and came toward Jesus.** Peter uses the word **"If,"** seeking reassurance. However, wouldn't the Lord's sheep recognize His voice? Yet, the Lord does not respond with rebuke; instead, He offers Peter grace.

How frequently does the Lord provide clear guidance, yet we still struggle with doubt and unbelief? We often wrestle with uncertainties, thinking, "Lord, I know I've heard you multiple times and understood the sermon, but I just need one more sign." Instead, let us thank our gracious and merciful Lord for His guidance and patience. The Lord welcomes our questions, even when many feel too intimidated to ask. "Lord, I feel you calling me to this task, but could you confirm it? Please send a sign or reassurance that this is indeed your will."

How often do you address your doubts and need reassurance? When will we fully recognize His patience, mercy, and grace, and give Him the glory and honor He deserves? Despite our doubts, insecurities, and fears, He still permits us to seek affirmation from Him.

Peter is remembered as the only other person to walk on water, empowered by God's supernatural strength. This incredible event happened because he was willing to go beyond his comfort zone.

Think about the extraordinary things that could occur if you hear God say, **"Come,"** and find the courage to step into the unknown. I recognize your fears and uncertainties, and that you don't have all the answers. God doesn't reveal the entire path from start to finish because, if He did, faith wouldn't be necessary. Some doors open only when we take a leap of faith, and specific opportunities come by stepping out in trust.

Matthew 14:30-31, *But when he saw the strength of the wind, he was afraid, and beginning to sink, he cried out, "Lord, save me!" Immediately Jesus reached out his hand, caught hold of him, and said to him,* "You of little faith, why did you doubt?" Peter walks on water, held up by the Lord's divine strength, with his focus on

Jesus. Whatever the Lord asks of you, He will help as long as you keep your gaze on Him. But if you turn your attention to pride, arrogance, distractions, negative influences, or hardships—and look away from Christ— you start to sink.

Distancing yourself from the Lord can lead to declines in your mind, heart, life, and relationships. The only outcome of disconnecting from Christ is a further descent—you fall deeper. His love is what makes you sing and reminds you that you can't face life relying solely on your strength; it would be unkind of Him to let you stray and still thrive. You might experience emptiness and notice that things aren't as they once were, yet this separation persists. You have turned away from His body and lost sight of Him. Nevertheless, remember that the Lord did not let Peter drown.

During moments of crisis, lengthy speeches are futile; what truly matters is being honest with the Lord Jesus. I am in pain, Lord; please help me. I am struggling and feel lost. I have stumbled again—please assist! Remember, He values sincerity and passion in your prayers. Your pleas should be heartfelt and genuine.

Whenever you falter on God's path, He will raise you up again. Each time you face challenges within His will, He will lift you once more.

The main message is that Jesus walking on water demonstrates His divine nature as God incarnate. This passage urges us to see Jesus clearly for who He truly is, focusing on Him rather than Peter. He remains the central figure throughout every verse. The key point for you is that true victory in any challenge isn't just about surviving. Real triumph comes from deepening your understanding of Jesus's majesty and His presence in your life. Your strongest testimony is everything you've overcome. It's not based on your strength but on Christ's power working through you. It's Yahweh's strength within you, the One who has delivered you and shown His mercy.

How often has He forgiven you? How many times has He extended His grace? The true miracle is our ongoing growth in understanding His true nature. What significance does a testimony hold if it isn't centered on Christ? How did you come to see Him as your Savior if He hadn't rescued you from darkness at some point?

God allows storms mainly for correction and growth. The storm that sent Jonah was intended to redirect him when he was heading the wrong way. Similarly, storms in believers' lives are meant to strengthen faith and deepen knowledge of God's character. When facing challenges that God permits—those not caused by your sin or disobedience—remember that these difficulties occur even when you are aligned with His will, obedient, and doing your best. These storms—trials, hardships, and conflicts—are under the Lord's guidance.

Jesus was led into the wilderness, so the Lord most likely has led you there for a reason. The Lord prays for you in **John 17:9,** "I pray for them. I am not praying for the world but for those you have given me, because they are yours." And in **Romans 8:28**, *We know that all things work together for the good of those who love God, who are called according to his purpose.*

The Lord will come to you even if His presence feels distant now, like your prayers go unanswered and bounce off the ceiling. Trust that He is listening. If you're in a storm, He allows, He will reach out to you.

Over time, you'll notice His presence, find comfort, and feel surrounded by Him. He approaches you. Reading the scriptures can help you realize that He communicates through His Word. The Lord will support your growth. As you handle challenges effectively, each one shapes and strengthens you. He is transforming your character, faith, confidence, and trust. He will assist in your development. So, challenges are not just obstacles but also growth opportunities.

The Lord will guide you. If He has brought you here, He will support you through it. Nothing that threatens to overwhelm your life is beyond His power to help you overcome. Keep progressing according to God's plan. Don't buy into the misconception of the American gospel that suggests walking with Jesus means facing no hardships. Instead, accept the biblical promise that you will encounter trials and challenges. Yet, take courage— I have overcome the world. Trust that I will lead you through these times, pray for you, provide comfort, support your growth, and guide you beyond obstacles.

Jesus, who was resurrected after death, assured us, *"I will never leave you nor forsake you."* Therefore, when facing a trial while following God's path, don't give up in despair. Instead, pause and pray, "Lord, you have brought me here. I thank you for praying for me and my community, as they support me. I feel your presence reaching out to me during this challenge. Even if I don't see it now, I trust that you will transform me through this experience. I am grateful that this situation is temporary; you will lead me to the other side with a deeper understanding of who you are and a greater awareness of my need for you."

CHAPTER 28

PRAYER

Eternal Father, many of our sons and daughters face
challenges such as conflicts, financial struggles, and
bad news. Some of us may currently enjoy peace, but
unknowingly, a storm is on the horizon. Thank you,
Lord, for your Word. I pray for all our brothers and
sisters, in your Son's name, to stand firm in this truth:
you are the bread of life, the Son of God, who never
abandons us. You reach out to us through life's trials
and turbulent seas, showing your authority over the
devil and revealing your greatness, glory, and power. I

pray for our spiritual growth; as we face difficulties, may we grow closer to you, with greater trust and more profound reverence. We will not use scripture or Christianity for self-glorification but will always view Jesus as the hero of every story. Strengthen our love for you; help us cherish what you cherish and detest what you detest. Remove all idols from our hearts. Be Lord over our minds and hearts. Jesus, help us recognize your grace amid our flaws, and keep us in awe of who you are; just hearing your name should make us weak in the knees. In your loving name, we pray. Amen.

CHAPTER 29

TESTIFY

What is a testimony? When do they typically happen? How do they impact people's lives? A testimony is an account of God's divine interventions in human lives, as personally witnessed. They mainly occur at two key moments: when an individual says, **"I was once lost but now I am found."**

If you've moved from darkness into light, from death to life, or if you once felt God's wrath but now know His perfect love—and your eyes have been opened to God's truth in heaven, comprehending why you've embraced the Savior's grace—then you have a story to tell. Your story might be summarized as: **"I was distant from God, but now I am saved."** Even if you grew up in church and are now saved, your name is recorded in the Lamb's Book of Life. You hold a testimony.

Testimonies emerge when God's grace, goodness, and power intersect with human experiences during adversity, trouble, and trials. Each encounter with God's grace in such moments becomes a testimony as we come through them. Reflecting on your life since salvation and noting every instance where God's goodness has connected with your journey helps you recognize and count these testimonies. How do testimonies impact people? For the speaker, sharing stories fosters feelings of empowerment and liberation, providing a sense of freedom. For the listener, it sparks hope, encourages faith, and helps build courage— showing that hearing testimonies plants a seed of belief.

Many of us have faced struggles for years or even decades, and I want to encourage you: no matter how long or challenging the journey, if Christ is involved, you will reach the other side. Even if the results are not immediate and only seen in eternity, being in Christ means holding onto a hope that surpasses this life. It was Paul who said in **Romans 5:3-5,** *And not only that, but we also boast in our afflictions, because we know that affliction produces endurance, endurance produces proven character, and proven character produces hope.*

This hope will not fail us because God's love has been poured into our hearts through the Holy Spirit, who was given to us. Nothing in life should diminish your praise and testimony. The devil needs to realize he cannot harm you here. We should not fear death, as the enemy's actions cannot erase our testimony. Christ will be glorified on every mountain and valley; even in death, His name will be exalted.

We should devote our minds, souls, hearts, and strength to serving God. Remember that some recognized Jesus as the Messiah based on others' testimonies. History shows how Christ transformed the life of an unnamed woman **(Matthew 9:20-22)**, who was so thrilled about their encounter and what He had done that she couldn't hide her excitement. After meeting Christ, she eagerly spread her testimony everywhere.

Malachi 4:2 states, ***But for you who fear my name, the 'sun of righteousness' will rise with healing in its wings, and you will go out and playfully jump like calves from the stall.*** The term 'SUN' here symbolizes the **"SON"**—the Son of God. The scripture indicates that healing will come from him when Christ returns. In Hebrew, **"wings"** refer to the edges of garments or tassels. Jewish tradition holds that touching the edge of the Messiah's garment can bring healing, aligning with the prophecy that healing will be in his wings upon the arrival of the Son of Righteousness.

Matthew 9:22, For the woman whom Jesus healed, he addressed her, "Have courage, daughter. Your faith has saved you."

What about your testimony? When was the last time you felt rescued? Reflect on each moment when He helped you overcome a challenge or made a way where there was none. Consider the lessons you're learning from Scripture and the emotions you experience in church, which you say you love. Think about the insights from last Sunday's sermon.

Many people around you face hopelessness; they don't believe in the God you serve and see Jesus as a punchline because that's how He's been portrayed. Yet, all of us have been saved—each time we encounter God's grace and power. So, why aren't we sharing these stories?

Many people are searching for hope, and your testimony can lead them to it. If you reveal that any part of your past has been used against you, remember the blood now covers it, turned into a weapon for Christ's glory. Share your daily salvation story and keep testifying to all the Lord is doing in your life, guiding you through every season, from glory to glory. Proclaim His salvation and make Christ known. Testify. Today, I pray the Spirit of evangelism is ignited in you, fueling your words and actions with passion. From now on, let your life be a continuous testimony of Christ's work— He lived, He died, He rose, and He saved me. This should be a regular part of your life. Testify.

CHAPTER 30

PRAYER

Father, in Jesus' name, I pray for those empowered by the Holy Spirit to escape darkness, asking you to ignite a passionate flame within them that shines through the Spirit's work. Please help us to be free from sin and all forms of immorality, preserving our testimony's purity and avoiding secret wrongdoings. Strengthen our love for you, holiness, and righteousness, and deepen our aversion to all ungodliness. Open our eyes to understand the season we're in and make us your voice; guide our actions so we can serve as your instruments—

sharing, singing, and proclaiming Jesus as our Lord and Savior. We will continually declare your name until you return. I ask for Your fire to fall upon our mouths and fingers, in your precious, holy name. Amen.

CHAPTER 31

KNOWING TRUTH

In the United States, people often trust apostles, prophets, and individuals more than the word of God. Historically, many influential men and women of God in the body of Christ have struggled with contradictions. Their public behaviors often do not match their private actions; they preach principles from the pulpit that they do not practice in their personal lives. This results in sermons filled with doctrine but lacking true righteousness. Those inwardly corrupt maintain a facade of piety, and we frequently idolize them based on their public image, unaware of the darkness they hide privately. Today's key issues in America are authority and authenticity, which are the foundation of our values and the measures we use to judge credibility.

Learning to discern is essential. Relying on God's word rather than human statements—whether from a pastor, preacher, bishop, or prophet—helps prevent feelings of guilt caused by others' words, even when spoken by a man or woman of God at a conference. As a result, you avoid feeling guilty for responsibilities that the Lord never actually assigned to you. These doctrines are misleading and hidden behind the phrase ***"God said."***

They are baseless theological assertions lacking scriptural support. How often have you heard a preacher on social media say, ***"God said,"*** only to endorse a law they try to enforce that isn't rooted in God's word? Many people may have encountered messages from churches, books, conferences, or individuals claiming to speak on God's behalf, which can evoke feelings of guilt about behaviors, rules, or practices that are difficult to follow. When you fail to meet these standards, that guilt is misplaced because the scriptures never required such expectations.

Example

The Lord said in **Luke 11:39,** "Now you Pharisees clean the outside of the cup and dish, but inside you are full of greed and evil."

Jesus frequently challenged societal norms and man-made rules established by corrupt individuals. He adhered to His Father's guidance, rejecting the religion and legalism imposed by those burdening God's Word with extra rules. We should strive to follow His example by resisting human regulations, legalism, and false doctrines that hinder our Christian walk. Many of you have adopted practices into your faith that are not supported by Scripture, often because you encountered them at conferences or from books. Someone mentioned that ignoring instructions upsets them. I hope more people find the courage to reject false doctrines made by humans.

Many may not realize they're being misled because they lack a personal understanding of the scriptures. This underscores the importance of reading and studying the Bible so that we can confidently identify errors and say, 'That's not right. No, the Lord didn't say that.' Isn't it tiring to hear people claim God spoke, yet their words contradict scripture? Reference **Galatians 1:1-9.** Why do you find yourself listening to voices who haven't read the Bible? Is it because of their fame, status, or social media influence?

Do you believe they have a unique connection with Christ that you haven't reached? Or do you think they receive messages from God that you can't hear? Could it be that their insights seem more profound than your understanding? Often, their eloquence makes their words seem like divine truth. Try shifting your admiration from polished speeches to authentic character, honest actions, and biblical truth. Be wary of false prophets who might mislead God's followers.

Many people find the word ineffective because they follow teachings not rooted in the Bible. Although the Pharisees were corrupt, we often behave in similar ways, setting up our own rules to sidestep God's commandments. When faced with the challenges of God's Word, we frequently create internal laws to avoid

His directives. In essence, we carve out safe spaces for sin and compromise.

We come across scriptures that say, "be holy before you get married," but this can feel inconvenient because of love for your partner. So, you may set your own rules to bypass God's commandments. The scripture also instructs us to forgive, yet when the pain is deep, you might create a personal law to withhold forgiveness, avoiding God's guidance. Similarly, although scripture promotes generosity, the involvement of your money might lead you to develop a mindset that sidesteps God's laws, and this pattern can repeat. When faced with complex ideas, instead of allowing them to inspire change, you may justify ignoring them by thinking, 'I can ignore that because...' This creates a mental refuge where your sins and compromises remain.

Jesus reminds us of **Matthew 7:22-23,** "On that day many will say to me, 'Lord, Lord, didn't we prophesy in your name, drive out demons in your name, and do many miracles in your name?' Then I will announce to them, I never knew you. Depart from me, you lawbreakers!' This is for the individual who embraces sin.

God is calling you from heaven to wake up. Now is the moment to live authentically and pursue holiness. Seek me with all your heart. Remember the passage that states neither the sexually immoral, nor the homosexual, nor those who partake in idolatry or divination will inherit the Kingdom of Heaven.

God opposes sin, and experiencing conviction is a positive sign. It signifies that your heart remains connected to God. Each time conviction occurs, it's an invitation from the Lord to draw closer to Him, revealing His love for you more clearly. **Matthew 15:7-9,** Hypocrites! Isaiah prophesied correctly about you when he said: This people honors me with their lips, but their heart is far from me. They worship me in vain, teaching as doctrines human commands". Followers are not following the one who sees everything.

If your words and actions don't align, everything loses meaning. When there's a gap between what you say, post, and how you live, you risk appearing hypocritical. Jesus said, "If you love me, obey my commandments," highlighting that love and obedience are connected through God's law. Continuing to depend on your own laws can make it difficult to forgive others. You might feel no need to be generous with your resources. As you focus on sticking to your self-made rules, you justify your behavior with reasoning. Consequently, you build many barriers—areas in your life where God's word has little influence.

American Christians often overlook a crucial aspect: their witness. This impacts how others see, feel about, and interpret them. Many don't realize that building their witness takes years, but it can be lost in an instant. It reflects the authenticity of their faith. Although many attend church and sin, they do so out of apathy toward their Christian witness. Without harmony in life, no anointing or authority can be carried in words. How many people avoid God just because they dislike us? They see God as a joke because His followers sometimes appear to be one. We attend church on Sundays, but then pursue our desires.

Time passes quickly. The Lord sacrificed His life for you, shedding His blood to save you—all for your benefit. He has rescued you, saving you from hell—a feat you could never achieve on your own. Despite all He has done, our most common form of hypocrisy is often our response. How can we acknowledge Jesus' sacrifice and still fail to truly turn away from the cross, giving our lives completely on this altar?

Superficial American Christianity promotes a compromise, making it easy to tolerate sin rather than pursue holiness. There is a better, more anointed, and discerning version of yourself waiting to be revealed. When you pray, God listens because the prayers of the righteous have power. You might think, "I've been praying; He hasn't responded." But the scripture says, ***"If you love iniquity, He will not answer your prayers,"*** because of your love for sin.

Isaiah 59:2, *"But your iniquities are separating you and your God, and your sins have hidden His face from you so that He does not listen."* It emphasizes that harboring sin in your heart—loving sin—causes the Lord to ignore your prayers. You may wonder why your pleas go unanswered, while the prayers of the righteous carry great power. May the Lord fill you with a deep desire for sincerity, a genuine heart, and a passionate commitment to Jesus with all your soul.

Each morning, aim to honor the Lord. If you notice flaws in yourself, hear words that clash with your values, or have improper desires, confess them to the Lord. Whatever the issue, bring it to Him. Jesus said, ***"My son, my daughter, you've dedicated your life to me, but you're still facing struggles on the lower shelf. Inside you is immense strength—whether you're a woman or a man, you're resilient. You have no idea of the remarkable things I could achieve through you if you truly live for me sincerely. Give me your genuine self and your heart, and watch how I change your life. Just wait and see what I can do."***

CHAPTER 32

PRAYER

Dear Lord, I pray for an intense outpouring of conviction, repentance, and a profound longing for holiness and righteousness. Let there be a process of breaking, washing, cleansing, and purging that drives your people to crave more profound spiritual experiences—not just sermons or temporary feelings. They should feel the urgency as time slips away and respond to your call to achieve something meaningful, striving to become better versions of themselves—those who turn from sin, follow your laws, cherish your scriptures, and dedicate their hearts to you. May we passionately pursue you wholeheartedly, in the name of your Son, Jesus. Amen

CHAPTER 33

UNCLEAN

In the New Testament, Christ redefines purity from external appearances to internal qualities. During His first sermon, he proclaimed, "Blessed are the pure in heart; they shall see God." After encountering Him and understanding His sacrifices, you'll relate to Paul, who said, *"I am torn. Half of me wants to be with the Lord, which is far better. Yet, I feel compelled to stay and fulfill my mission here, knowing others need to hear the gospel."* As you deepen your relationship with the Lord, you may develop a distaste for the flesh.

All the pain you've caused others—such as insecurities, hang-ups, self-condemnation, self-criticism, and struggles with shame—stems from your heart. It originates from your sinful nature and flows from within. I recognize the scripture's view that the heart is wicked and deceitful. Yet, the vital question is: who truly understands it? Your heart can deceive you.

We should desire for God to examine our hearts and recognize His image within us. We should hope that God searches our hearts and understands His commandments. Our longing should be for God to look into our hearts and find someone who hates sin; when anti-Christ thoughts come to mind, we should strive to keep our hearts pure and unblemished.

Matthew 15:10-11, Summoning the crowd, he told them, "Listen and understand. It's not what goes into the mouth that defiles a person, but what comes out of the mouth- that defiles a person." I encourage you to avoid hypocrisy and to prioritize honesty, authenticity, and reality. Your words should match your actions. Jesus emphasizes protecting people from false teachings, which is why he criticizes the Pharisees. Therefore, what comes from the heart can make someone unclean. Your words can define who you are; everything you say influences your identity. What you share reveals your true self, giving insight into your genuine nature through your posts and comments. So, what is truly coming from your heart?

Who takes offense at the truth? Usually, it's hypocrites—those who feel uncomfortable or inconsistent with it. Deceitful individuals often react negatively to honesty. Many of us are cautious when communicating with others, hesitant to share particular messages for fear of offending. Brothers and sisters, don't avoid sharing the Gospel, even if it might offend some.

Why do we try to sanitize the Scriptures? The gospel can be challenging to accept. Are you aware of what it reveals about us? It shows that we are sinners, born in sin, and separated from God. The Scriptures also state that unless you are born again, you are considered an enemy of God; He has issues with you.

1 Thessalonians 5:9, *For God did not appoint us to wrath, but to obtain salvation through our Lord Jesus Christ.* We must reach out to atheists and others who are unaware of Christ or do not live for Him. Although God's love extends to all humanity, Paul emphasizes that until a person is saved, they are considered objects of wrath. Share the truth, even if it offends, since the gospel's good news can be challenging because it uncovers our sinfulness.

Psalm 51:5, *Indeed, I was guilty when I was born; I was sinful when my mother conceived me.* This is why we all need a savior. Everyone born into sin needs Jesus. On judgment day, when the Lord evaluates us against the 10 commandments, no one will pass without Christ. The Lord will judge the entire world based on His moral law. The Ten Commandments serve as guidance for this judgment, highlighting humanity's need for a Savior.

Valuing anything more than God means breaking the first commandment. Envying others also breaches this commandment. If you've ever felt jealous of someone, you've committed a transgression. Stealing what isn't yours also breaks this rule. Avoid giving false testimony; lying already violates this commandment. Comparing yourself to this moral standard highlights your difficult situation. That's why we need Christ — He is the only one who fully kept the law. He lived a perfect life in His mind, thoughts, and heart. Since He never broke the law, He could die sacrificially, exchanging His righteousness for your unrighteousness so you, as a sinner, can be justified before God.

Righteousness isn't based on good deeds or church attendance. True righteousness is only found in Christ, where, upon examining us through the Ten Commandments, God sees Christ living within us. Consequently, when He looks at His son or daughter, He considers them 'righteous.' That's why we should love, adore, and exalt Christ, both as lovers and as His proclaimers: when my Father in heaven sees me as righteous, it is because I am clothed in Christ.

Matthew 15:13, He replied, "Every plant that my heavenly father didn't plant will be uprooted." The Lord declared, *"Leave them be. Do not worry. In the end, my Father will uproot all who do not belong to me."* This shows that you cannot deceive God. You may try to hide, but eventually, the Lord will bring about separation. It urges you to stop playing God and to stop thinking you're safe just because you go to church.

It urges you to turn away from false religion, moralism, and legalism. Instead, it invites you to come to Christ as He draws you closer. Remember, tomorrow is not guaranteed; today is the right time to accept salvation. Humbly approach the altar and pray, ***"Lord, forgive me for my sins."*** This act can lead to redemption and reflects Christ's unconditional love, reminding you how often this call is extended. Now is the time to surrender—trust in me and see what I can do with your life.

Matthew 15:14, "Leave them alone! They are blind guides. And if the blind guide the blind, both will fall into a pit." All false teachers—such as apostles, evangelists, pastors, prophets, and leaders like Mormon figures, Joseph Smith, and Muhammad are now buried.

The only exception is Jesus, whose remains remain undiscovered. When teachers lack proper guidance and are supported by followers who are misled, the consequences can be lasting. It is crucial to focus on accurate teachings and sound doctrine while rejecting false doctrines. A misinformed teacher often makes every sermon about the listener, portraying them as the main character in biblical stories and turning scriptural narratives into personal stories. Their messages tend to focus on motivation and positivity, mainly to evoke emotional responses.

They often quote scripture out of context to fill a 45-minute talk based on their preferences. Throughout this discussion, the focus shifts entirely to you, heavily emphasizing self-help and narcissism. This creates an image of an imaginary God and a fictional Jesus in your mind. As a result, your prayers become centered on yourself. You start to believe that Christianity is about you, that the Bible speaks to your personal needs, and that God made you to serve Him.

How many Christians have voiced frustration toward God for not answering their prayers? The real reason might be that you've embraced a version of Christianity that isn't aligned with scripture. God didn't create you for self-focus; instead, He designed you to serve Him. Once you understand this, your prayers will shift. They become: Lord, what do You want me to do? Lord, transform my heart. Lord, open my eyes. Lord, increase Your anointing in my life. Lord, help me find opportunities to share the gospel. What is Your purpose for me?

You should sincerely pursue inner change to become a more impactful witness and a better disciple. You cry out, "Lord, let your Kingdom come and your will be done on earth." You pray for the unreached, especially those in the East under Islamic strongholds. Ask Jesus to continue revealing Himself to them, to win their hearts, love them, deliver them, and save them.

Matthew 15:15-20, Then Peter said, "Explain the parable to us." "Do you still lack understanding?' he asked. "Don't you realize that whatever goes into the mouth passes into the stomach and is eliminated? But what comes out of the mouth comes from the heart, and this defiles a person. For from the heart comes evil thoughts, murderers, adulteries, sexual immoralities, thefts, false testimonies, slander. These are the things that defile a person; but eating with unwashed hands does not defile a person."

Jesus emphasizes that moral concerns about your diet do not make you unclean. You are free to eat anything you desire. He teaches that the real source of harm and ruin is in your heart. The negative tendencies that damage humanity originate from within and cannot be fixed by human effort alone. It is essential to recognize that sanctification must come from the Lord, through the Holy Spirit working within you. You cannot fix your heart simply by moral actions or good behavior; only Christ can change it.

Jesus taught that harboring hate is like murdering someone in your heart. If you've ever felt hate, it's as if you've taken another person's life. Such emotions corrupt you and make you appear like a foul sewer in my eyes. So, what pollutes our hearts and minds, along with our wicked thoughts? Both physical and emotional acts of murder stain the heart. Adultery also defiles the heart, and it's not only about the physical act. Jesus said that even looking at someone with lust equates to committing adultery. I want you to love the Lord. Jesus doesn't want you to have a defiled heart.

I genuinely want you to wholeheartedly pursue Christ—loving, obeying, and striving to live justly. Stay away from worldly temptations and vanity. Experience the beauty in holiness, purity, and the Spirit's life. Each morning, I hope you wake up feeling Jesus's presence as you dedicate your life to Him. Throughout the day, I wish for you to have moments with Christ, trusting He recognizes your efforts to live rightly.

When you lie down at night, feel the comfort of Christ's presence, with His voice loving and embracing you. May He reveal insights through the Word. Find a quiet place to bask in His presence. My deepest wish is that you love Him profoundly. I want you to recognize social injustices on platforms like social media, which should evoke feelings of sorrow and a desire to pray.

While shopping at the grocery store, I hope you pray for those who are lost. As you walk, feel a deep concern for those far from God. I see you as an instrument that God can use at any moment. My hope is for you to be someone anointed for His service, ready to follow wherever He leads, no matter the circumstances. I wish for you to be trusted by Him with resources, revelations, truth, and insight. I want you to be powerful and demonstrate strong character. My desire is for you to embody integrity as a woman and to be virtuous. Above all, I hope what lies within you becomes your most beautiful trait.

Chapter 34

Prayer

Dear Heavenly Father, we acknowledge your greatness, power, and worthiness. Thank You for your Son, through whom many have been delivered from darkness into His glorious light. You have removed our depravity and chosen us as your elect. You have redeemed those you are reconciling to yourself before judgment falls. We understand that our fight is not against flesh and blood but against spiritual forces. We praise you for the Spirit alive within the church and us. We honor the warring angels and recognize you as the

Lord of hosts, the commander of heaven's armies, with heaven's full support behind your church and body on earth. We entrust ourselves to you, confident that you will return for a spotless bride, and we pray to be part of that bride by faith. We oppose every demonic force and declare, "Satan, the Lord rebuke you," in the mighty name of Jesus Christ, our Lord and Savior.

CHAPTER 35

MIXED FEELINGS OF LOVE

Love is the most powerful emotion we encounter in life. The Bible teaches that perfect love casts out all fear. Yet, when love is still growing or immature, fear can hold it back, hinder it, or even harden it, sometimes blocking it entirely. Nothing we face right now compares to what the Lord has prepared for all His sons and daughters.

Love can be both beautiful and painful.

Sometimes, God's plan involves us enduring hardships during specific seasons to achieve His purposes. Just as

Jesus was on the brink of accepting His Father's will—facing persecution from His creation—He was ready to be persecuted by those He had made. He prepared to submit to His Father's unwelcome and challenging plan. As followers of Christ, we must ask ourselves if we are willing to submit to God's will to the same degree. Can we trust and obey even when His plans are complex or unwanted? Are we ready to accept suffering for His sake, loving Him enough to endure for the Lamb of God?

As loyal followers, we must not ignore the truth by accepting comforting lies or listening to false prophets who promote sin. Instead, we are called to live wholeheartedly and to endure suffering for the Lord Jesus Christ. Can you submit to His will, even if it conflicts with your own? Jesus is telling His disciples that He will be leaving them soon. He advises them to let go of their attachment to physical intimacy because he knows he will soon be taken away from them forever on earth. He will be removed, return for 40 days, then depart again.

Currently, he uses his words to help them detach from their physical connection as he prepares to leave and send the Holy Spirit to guide them. **Matthew 16:21,** ***From then on Jesus began to point out to his disciples that it was necessary for him to go to Jerusalem and suffer many things from the elders, chief priests, and scribes, be killed, and be raised the third day.*** He will later tell them that I am no longer with you, but I will send a helper: the Holy Spirit, the Paraclete. He is the only one who comes alongside you, speaks to you, guides, leads, reminds, rebukes, and empowers. He is not an 'it' or just a force, as some false religions claim. He is the third person of the Trinity, part of God's divine nature.

John noted that Jesus referred to the Holy Spirit as 'He' in his account. We believe in one God existing as three persons: God the Father, God the Son, and God the Spirit. The Lord uses language here to downplay their physical connection to him, as he prepares to leave. Jesus reveals the imminent fulfillment of the gospel, emphasizing his death on the cross. He warns that he will soon complete his mission by being nailed to the cross to bear all your sins—past, present, and future. He is on the brink of fulfilling the gospel message that has been foretold for thousands of years.

Without it, humanity remains captive to sin and cannot access forgiveness. The absence of the cross means there is no sufficient righteousness to stand before a holy God. Our deeds and righteousness are never enough. Without the cross, forming an authentic relationship with God the Father becomes impossible. Sadly, some Christians, due to familiarity and pride, have become desensitized and now lack joy in the message of the cross.

By staying connected to His word and truly following Him as His disciples, we gain understanding of the truth—the truth of what happened on that cross. We recognize the righteousness that has been credited to us. I will quietly thank God for all He has done, especially my salvation. If you value your salvation, praise Him. Tears for Him show gratitude for how the Lord has led you from darkness into light. When you couldn't do it alone, those tears were a sign of joy.

What saddens me most is the large number of people around me who are lost without salvation. Those caught in sin will endure eternal separation from God. In the American church, we also witness the foolishness of both men and women, along with idolatry, incorrect teachings, and wasted time.

Mark states in 9:32, *But they did not understand this statement, and they were afraid to ask him.* They refuse to accept the Lord's prophecy about the most crucial event in human history: the death and resurrection of Christ. These events mark a significant split in time, giving rise to the BC (Before Christ) and AD (Anno Domini, in the year of our Lord) periods. Our calendar is based on these defining moments. Therefore, writing 2025 signifies that 2025 years have passed since Christ's resurrection.

Paul emphasized that without Christ's resurrection, our beliefs hold no meaning. Everything is pointless if Christ did not rise. Only one person beyond all religions is not confined to a grave. The disciples failed to understand his mission; he rose on the third day and now sits at the right hand of God the Father. Jesus predicted this pivotal event in human history.

When Jesus spoke of the Son of Man rising, they should have understood the message. However, their naive affection led them to believe the Roman government wouldn't be overthrown and that their time with Him was ending. Their love for Jesus made them wish for His continued presence, but they missed the fact that He would be resurrected. Instead, their emotions blinded them to God's faithful promise.

They had the Old Testament and should have understood that Christ would come, live, suffer, die, be buried for three days, and rise again. Christ would establish His reign. Yet, despite their familiarity with the Old Testament, their emotions at that moment overwhelmed their understanding. In that instant, their feelings took precedence over the truth of God's Word.

Matthew 17:23, They will kill Him, and on the third day He will be raised up. And they were deeply distressed.

We share this fault. We sometimes let our feelings during certain seasons or moments cloud the truth in God's word. Yet, there comes a point when we must dedicate ourselves to the Bible. Remember, even in times of feeling abandoned, the word comforts us with the promise that He will never leave nor forsake us. I realize we may sometimes feel He is unresponsive, but Scripture assures us that He hears the cries of His righteous children.**2 Corinthians 10:5,** *And every* *proud thing that is raised up against the* *knowledge of God, and we take every thought* *captive to obey Christ.*

When the devil tricks you, return to what the Word says. If your emotions are unsettled, recall what the Scripture states. When you feel unloved, focus on what the Word indicates. If you perceive a lack of support, reflect on what the Bible asserts. And if your life isn't turning out as hoped or circumstances aren't ideal, consider what the Word teaches. Remember: the struggles we face now are minor compared to the glory that will be revealed to those in Christ Jesus. Although we may encounter difficulties temporarily, a future awaits where tears, sickness, and pain will disappear— a life that Jesus Christ has prepared for us.

Reflect on the word and know that your Father fully understands you. Referencing **Psalm 139:14,** I will praise you because I have been remarkably and wondrously made. Your works are wondrous, and I know this very well.

Understanding the future shapes your present life. The Old Testament contains prophets sharing messages about what awaits the children of Israel, emphasizing the need for disciplined listening. Likewise, the New Testament, through Jesus Christ's teachings and the Book of Revelation, reveals upcoming events to His followers. God aims for His children to grasp His plans, which is why He gave a detailed scripture centered on the future. I believe the Lord is preparing to create a new world filled with new trees, pure water, and free from evil, death, suffering, pain, and sin.

This conviction inspires me to live for Christ and share His message with others, aiming for their salvation. My faith is grounded in my knowledge of God's word. Jesus will return for a church without blemish or wrinkle.

CHAPTER 36

PRAYER

Father God, we lift your holy name in praise and magnify you. We exalt you and your Son. Lord, we feel the wind of eternity surrounding us. We acknowledge that time is short, with a clock ticking backwards until Your Son's return. Thank you for the work you're doing among us—calling sons and daughters to yourself. As we wield the sword and sickle of your Word, we harvest souls into your eternal storehouse. Father, grant Your strength to uplift your servant and let your Spirit move powerfully in the hearts of your people as your Word is shared. May the truth have a profound impact on everyone—believers, atheists, and skeptics alike—stirring deep emotions and thoughts. We pray for ongoing transformation into the likeness of your Son, asking that you change our hearts. All this we pray in the name of our Lord and Savior, Jesus Christ. Amen.

CHAPTER 37

TAKE A STEP BACK

Believers in biblical Christianity receive the greatest blessing of freedom through Christ. Once under God's wrath and separated from Him, Jesus' sacrifice has brought you near the Father. You are now free from God's anger. Previously enslaved by demonic spirits, Christ's blood has liberated you from their control. You believed lies in your mind, but God's Word has broken those strongholds, enabling you to walk in freedom through Jesus' truth. Today, we walk together as followers of Christ, enjoying a special freedom in serving the Lord Jesus. Only immature believers operate in this freedom and lack the wisdom to restrain themselves when it might cause unnecessary offense to others.

You can stand firm on doctrine whenever you wish. However, if you find yourself in a theological disagreement over a non-essential issue that could offend someone, wisdom indicates you've been emphasizing freedom too strongly. While we are free from false religions, offending others over non-ethical customs requires restraint. Despite the extraordinary freedom given to us in Christ's body, only immature believers fail to recognize when to exercise restraint and temper.

Matthew 17:24-26 *When they came to Capernaum, those who collected the temple tax approached Peter and said, "Doesn't your teacher pay the temple tax?" "Yes," he said. When he went into the house, Jesus spoke to him first,* *"What do you think, Simon? From whom do earthly kings collect tariffs or taxes? From their sons or from strangers?"* *"From stranger," he said.* *"Then the sons are free,"* *Jesus told him.*

The Lord knew even before Peter voiced his concerns, showing that nothing in our lives is hidden from Him. No pain or hardship escapes His awareness. Rather than avoiding our struggles, Jesus intentionally seeks them out, illustrating His love through active engagement. During times when prayer seems impossible and tears, confusion, or worries engulf me, I am grateful to serve a Messiah who fully understands my experiences. Even in moments when praying is difficult, His presence draws nearer to my pain.

Jesus asked him this question to correct him, as He doesn't allow His disciples to hold false theology. The Lord loves you so much that He stops you from embracing wrong beliefs. Everything happening in the temple is meant to guide people toward a king, and now Christ is that King, the Son of God. All the temple's events point to Him. As Jesus said earlier in Matthew, He is greater than the temple. So, if you're collecting offerings to support a house for a king, and He owns that house, then He is not obligated to pay the tax.

Jesus clarifies to Peter, saying, *"I don't owe the tax because it is meant for the worship of who I am: God the Messiah."* As God in the flesh, Jesus is not subject to this tax. His followers, being followers of Christ, are also exempt.

Jesus told Peter, *"Since you've already told them I pay taxes, and although I am free, let's show grace on a minor issue. It's unnecessary to argue or fight over small matters. Paying this tax won't damage our witness, but causing unnecessary offense will. These men don't see that I am the Son of God, and you don't need to offend them just because they collect taxes for my Father's house."* **Matthew 17:27,** But, so we won't offend them, go to the sea, cast in a fishhook, and take the first fish that you catch. When you open its mouth you'll find a coin. Take it and give it to them for me and you."

The Lord indicates that we already carry a message that could be seen as offensive—the gospel. It declares that we are sinners, separated from God, and in need of salvation. On its own, this message can be offensive. Because it is inherently provocative, He does not want His followers to be unnecessarily offensive in society over minor issues. I encourage you not to say or post offensive things without a genuine reason. If someone is offended, it should be for a meaningful purpose, not over trivial matters. Exercising restraint with your speech and actions is essential.

God shows that those who serve Him will always have their needs fulfilled. The real challenge is our tendency to fixate only on the outcome. Often, God doesn't disclose the result beforehand; instead, He offers guidance that leads us there, helping us grow as we follow His path. Many of us frequently ask God for different needs, wondering, "Lord, why aren't You showing up here?" But the actual question is whether we are listening to His guidance.

He communicates His guidance through the Bible, offering ways to live your best life. Often, we complain about what we lack and neglect His advice. Ignoring reading, studying, and obeying can cause us to miss His plans for us. As you begin to follow His guidance, you'll notice opportunities and doors opening in your life. He will lead you to specific situations and tasks in your business or ministry as you obey Him. Additionally, He will provide the initial resources you need. Remember, He didn't just give Peter a coin; He provided detailed instructions. To see real change, start by obeying His Word.

We all owe a debt, but Christ, who owes nothing, has paid it in full. Jesus took on our sin. Matthews highlights the core message of the gospel: those who owed debts were set free, and a man owing nothing paid what was due. This serves as a constant reminder that this Messiah came, lived sinlessly, freed us from the law's burdens, died the death we deserved, rose on the third day, and paid the price to save us from God's wrath. How should we respond? We might attend church and drop a penny in the offering plate, but the proper response to our debt's payment is to live a life of complete surrender.

Our only response to debt being paid is to live in complete homage, worship, surrender, and service to Lord Jesus Christ. Lord, I allow Your Word to influence every part of my life—my mind, heart, actions, finances, marriage, parenting, and friendships. I release worldly concerns and fully surrender to you. My will is fully aligned with yours.

If you frequently feel anger toward God for unanswered prayers but haven't fully surrendered your life to Him, it indicates you're mainly seeking validation rather than authentic spiritual growth. You desire affirmation as wonderful, but may resist messages about repentance, surrender, or turning to the Messiah who died for you, possibly thinking, "I trust you because of your sacrifice. Here is my entire life in response."

Some people prefer to focus solely on blessings.

The Lord speaks to us through the Bible: 'My child, stop causing unnecessary offense.' During conflicts, I draw near. My corrections of your mistaken theology are driven by love, not judgment, because I don't want you defending me with falsehoods. You owed an unpayable debt— I have paid it for you. I am more than the Jewish figure you follow; I am the Son of God, the Messiah, the Almighty Christ. We should be saying, *"Jesus, I have given this to You. Jesus, I plan to change this for You. I will see this person differently for you. I surrender this to You." We must avoid just going through religious motions without truly surrendering our lives. When pride rises, ask yourself, "Could I pay that tax debt?"* NO.

A fulfilling life awaits beyond complete surrender, just as it does when you follow His guidance. Are you unintentionally offending others? Do you recognize when the Lord communicates with you through conflicts, grace, and mercy? Are you aware of His efforts to correct any misunderstandings about theology? Do you realize He has paid your debt? Are you fully surrendering every part of your life to Him? Is this merely about attending church, or is it genuinely about living a surrendered life to the Messiah?

CHAPTER 38

PRAYER

Dear Lord, please help us evaluate our freedom and recognize where we might unintentionally offend others. Guide us to be aware when you approach us during conflicts and open us to your correction regarding our thoughts, doctrines, or beliefs. Remind us to focus on what you accomplished on the cross— paying a debt we could never settle ourselves. I pray for sons and daughters whose lives are joyfully surrendered to you, declaring, ***"Lord, I surrender all to you. I commit to obeying your Word and***

following your ways, trusting that blessings and miracles will follow as we walk in obedience. Help us use our freedoms wisely and always remember the debt you paid." In your mighty name of Jesus Christ.

CHAPTER 39

SIN

The original sin that impacts all humans serves as the root of our life's challenges. It brings pain and suffering to society and is responsible for every tear of sorrow. It is the cause of tensions in relationships, friendships, and marriages. Moreover, this sin underpins many global issues we see today. Throughout history, sin has caused the collapse of empires, corruption in governments, and has affected every facet of human existence. It has corrupted your entire being, influencing your intellect, emotions, desires, wants, longings, worldview, language, mouth, heart, and feelings—every part of who you are.

Every individual and every aspect of you has been affected by sin. It represents the most significant obstacle in human existence, and I hate sin—both in myself and the church and society—not because I see myself as perfect, but because I understand the pain it causes. I know the destruction, heartbreak, and frustration it has brought into my life. I am not the only one who sees the damage sin causes; many moments in my past are marked by regrets related to it. There are parts of my story I wish I could undo because of the harm sin has done.

Matthew 18:7, Woe to the world because of offenses, For offenses will inevitably come, but woe to that person by whom the offense comes.

In his sermons, the Lord often uses the word 'woe' when addressing unrepentant sinners. It is a strongly solemn and impactful term—one you want to avoid. The Lord not only speaks this word himself but also emphasizes its seriousness by doubling it. Woe signifies an unavoidable punishment for the one it is directed at, indicating that something severe is coming.

Moreover, woe also conveys a deep sorrow from the heart.

Woe to the world because of temptations to sin. The Lord is emphasizing that He is judging the fallen human world. Woe to every government, role, and institution built by man that leads people into sin— such as corrupt governments, nations, America, and Planned Parenthood. The Lord declared, 'Woe to all man-made institutions that promote sin. This covers corrupt governments passing harmful laws, institutions, clinics, Planned Parenthood, and anyone involved in creating porn sites or sex trafficking—any entity that encourages sin in the world.' The Lord warned all entities and governments that act as channels for sin, saying, *"Woe to you."*

A harsh judgment awaits all who embody sin, and you should feel remorse for what you will endure because of your current actions. While sin is unavoidable in our fallen world, it is tragic to be the one responsible for its spread. Although we cannot wholly avoid sin, we must be careful not to act as catalysts that promote its expansion in society. Even though the world may be blinded by sin, I hope my children are not involved in or spreading it.

The Lord has existed eternally. In **Genesis 1:26,** it says, *'Make man in our image and likeness.'* He is an eternal existence who comprehends the damage caused by sin. The initial sin in the universe didn't happen in the Garden of Eden; it took place in heaven. Scripture tells us that, although God created many angelic beings, three archangels stand out: Michael, who leads in warfare; Gabriel, who delivers messages; and Lucifer, who is linked to worship.

The scripture mentions that his body was made from musical instruments and pipes, a lesson given by Ezekiel. Furthermore, **Isaiah 14** offers insights into Lucifer's time in heaven, indicating that he saw a reflection of his beauty, which sparked the first sin— pride—in his heart. The Bible states that this pride, along with excessive trading or prideful ambition, led to his corruption.

Lucifer began asserting himself to other angels, declaring his intent to surpass God. He told one angel, *'I'm going to be better than God,'* before repeating the same claim to others. He kept whispering about his ambition to outshine God to all these angels. This behavior resulted in his second sin and ignited a rebellion within him.

The scripture shows that he rebelled against God, leading to a war in heaven. Since dualism is not present, Satan is not more powerful than God Almighty. The scripture also mentions that Satan was expelled from heaven because of this rebellion. Moreover, Jesus said, "I saw Satan fall from heaven like lightning, down to the earth."

He is portrayed as the celestial dragon among the stars, leading one-third of the angels he deceived and influenced. Jude emphasizes that these angels left their heavenly dwelling and now face eternal punishment in fire for abandoning God. The fallen angels, cast out, are the demons that now inhabit the earth. An archangel who was demoted from their glory after becoming your adversary—namely, the devil and Satan.

The Lord acknowledges the deep harm that sin brings to human hearts and lives. He is aware of its destructive and catastrophic impact. He observes the pain we inflict on ourselves through sinful behaviors. When He looks at us, His heart is burdened with grief, especially as He sees His children who take pleasure in sin. He recognizes how sin damages our lives, destroys our witness, and weakens our credibility.

How often has the Lord responded to your tears with His love, yet He continues to watch over you as if expecting you to cease doing good? This is because the Lord understands the immense damage and destruction that sin brings into people's lives. He has taken extraordinary steps to warn His followers against engaging with sin carelessly.

Matthew 18:8, If your hand or your foot causes you to fall away, cut it off and throw it away. It is better for you to enter life maimed or lame than to have two hands or feet and be thrown into the eternal fire. The hand or foot represents sins like sowing discord, rebellion, lying, cheating, stealing, and harming others. The Lord stressed the importance of acknowledging, confronting, and removing all unrepentant sins. He calls for decisive action—doing whatever it takes to stop engaging in unrepentant sin. It is better to accept discipline and practice self-denial for correction than to risk hell by ignoring repentance.

Once you are genuinely saved, you remain saved. Those who endure to the end will be saved. You might think that saying a prayer or walking to the altar alone is sufficient to invite the Lord into your life and then live freely afterward. However, this is a deception from the enemy. He wrongly asserts that persistent sin causes the Lord to be silent and unaware. In truth, the Lord observes you and gently says, **'Son, daughter, you need to cease this.'** Address your sins firmly. Darkness in your life allows the devil to influence you, which is why I think having an accountability partner is crucial.

Matthew 18:9, And if your eye causes you to fall away, gouge it out and throw it away. It is better for you to enter life with one eye than to have two eyes and be thrown into hellfire.

Some believe that hell is just a metaphor, but Jesus emphasized it as a real place. He describes it as a physical location, though many misunderstand this. In the Sermon on the Mount, the eye symbolizes inner heart issues, representing hidden sins unseen by others but visible to God. These include unforgiveness, pride, lust, anger, jealousy, envy, greed, and self-importance.

Such sinful tendencies reside within the heart and remain concealed, similar to idolatry, which involves sins of the eyes and heart that are hidden from view. The Lord warns that when these issues are noticed, they should be removed.

Some individuals avoid addressing their sins because they believe grace excuses them. They assume that since we are in the age of grace and haven't experienced God's complete wrath against sin, they have permission to indulge in immoral behavior. Remind them of Ananias and Sapphira, whom God struck dead for their deceitfulness. **Acts 5:1-10**

If the Lord were to begin punishing people for their sins suddenly, I bet everyone would quickly change their ways. Do you know what this country has lost? Respect. Many believe God is just a joke, a name on a bracelet, and because He is holding back His anger, they think they can indulge in reckless behavior.

The Lord is urging His followers to uphold holiness every day, from Monday through Sunday. Many seek anointings but overlook the necessity of living a holy life; there is a cost involved in receiving an anointing. It's tiring to see people continually sing, preach, and post about holiness, yet not genuinely live holy lives. The Lord's command remains, *'Be holy, as I am.'*

The Lord sacrificially lived and died to take the punishment for our sins on the cross. He then rose from the dead and bestowed the Holy Spirit, which is Christ's power within us, enabling us to start anew. Understand the love of the Savior. You can turn from sin because He gives you the strength to lead a sinless life. If God's people do not take their Savior's words seriously, what credibility do we have before the world? If He told us to cut or pluck it out, He wouldn't ask us to do something beyond our ability. It's merely our excuses.

Father, in your holy name, deliver us from our justifications and the enemy's lies that suggest we must stay in sin. Remind us that we have the strength to live holy lives. Fill us with a reverent fear, Lord, so we can live righteously, committed to moral purity—challenging the sins within our hearts and lives—and maintain the integrity of our message to the world.

CHAPTER 40

PRAYER

Dear Heavenly Father, we come before you, praying that you draw us closer to yourself through Your Word. Help us look beyond our familiar readings so we can marvel at the truth, knowing that Christ is at the center of every verse. In our weakness, we rely on your strength. Christ, we long for a deeper relationship with you, and I ask you to fill us with encouragement and inspiration. Ignite passion in all your children's hearts. Please fill us with the Spirit of evangelism. Spirit of the living God, make us feel the burden of the world and move us through your truth to go out and proclaim your Son, Jesus Christ, to all. I pray this in your powerful, mighty name—our Lord and Savior, Jesus Christ. Amen.

CHAPTER 41

EVERYONE IS WORTH IT

Feeling worthless can be incredibly painful, especially when we believe that a mistake or hardship has caused us to fail and that we no longer matter to God. This intense emotion can cause followers of Christ to withdraw. Those who haven't experienced it might not notice our pain and could even make it worse through silence, negativity, or ridicule. When shame dominates, we expect support and kindness, but sometimes we're met with mockery, which intensifies our loneliness and deepens our feelings of insignificance.

Matthew 18:10, "See to it that you don't despise one of these little ones, because I tell you that in heaven their angels continually view the face of my Father in heaven."

The Lord's commandment is clear: it is not a suggestion. Do not look down on fellow Christians who are struggling with sin, facing challenging circumstances, or going through distress. When community members face hardships, stumble into sin, make mistakes, or drift away, do not despise them; the Spirit does not see others as lesser.

The Lord urges us to live together harmoniously, emphasizing the importance of honoring our brothers and sisters. Pray more frequently than judging, slandering, or criticizing others. Avoid harboring unjust hatred. Following Jesus' teachings helps cultivate love, acceptance, and a godly attitude. Although we are all made in God's image, we often forget others' worth and neglect their dignity. When the Lord uses 'For,' it indicates purpose or reason. Never look down on a brother or sister as if they are unworthy.

Jesus reveals an unseen realm where angelic beings advocate on our behalf. When we sin, make mistakes, or fall short, angels plead, saying, **"Lord, be merciful,"** and mention our names before the Father. *Acts 12:5, So Peter was kept in prison, but the church was praying fervently to God for him. Acts 12:7, Suddenly an Angel of the Lord appeared, and a light shone in the cell. Striking Peter on the side, he woke him up and said, "Quick, get up!" And the chains fell off his wrist.*

WHEN GOD GETS INVOLVED, CHAINS BREAK!!

Acts 12:11 describes how the Lord sent an angel to rescue Peter. This same act of divine intervention applies to you and me. God steps into situations beyond our ability to handle alone. The passage speaks to believers who have sinned, made mistakes, drifted away from the church, or face hardships. They might feel ashamed and withdraw. It is meant for believers in distress, reminding us not to judge them solely by their circumstances but to recognize that, despite their struggles, they are still precious to God.

Matthew 18:12, What do you think? If someone has a hundred sheep, and one of them goes astray, won't he leave the ninety-nine on the hillside and go and search for the stray?

Believers who have sinned, made mistakes, drifted from the church, or are facing difficulties might feel ashamed and retreat. This message is intended for believers in distress, reminding us that we often judge them by their circumstances rather than recognizing that, despite their struggles, they are still valuable to God.

The Lord uses imagery from Palestinian culture, depicting the people as sheep. Sheep often wander off and struggle to survive without a shepherd. They require someone to guide, nourish, and protect them, which is why they cannot thrive without this guidance. The Lord reminds those who stray that their sins, failures, and mistakes are severe enough that He will actively seek them out. He encourages us to adopt humility and childlike faith, urging the church to take a compassionate and pastoral stance. This attitude helps us to respond kindly when brothers and sisters drift away because of sin or mistakes, rather than neglecting them.

He discusses humble, childlike Christians going through tough times. As they drift from Christ due to feelings of guilt, shame, or unworthiness, we should work together to uplift them and counter those feelings so everyone can rise and glorify Him together, ensuring no one is left behind. Sometimes, simply being present can help someone come out of darkness by offering love and hope. God can use anyone at any moment to remind you of your worth and draw you back to Him. This reflects how He wants us to love one another.

If you notice a brother or sister going through a difficult time, overwhelmed by sin, and turning away from God in rebellion, reach out to offer support. Please send a message or call to remind them of their value.

Matthew 18:13, And if He Finds it, truly I tell you, He rejoices over that sheep more than over the ninety-nine that did not go astray. The word "if" signals an unsettling uncertainty: some individuals may not be located; some might turn away and never return. They could continue loving their sin until the end and face eternal separation. They may leave and follow another leader and congregation, and that's okay. Still, do your best to reach out and rescue the brother or sister who was once your friend, who is hurting, and who questions why they are straying. While you can't save everyone, your goal should be to keep the family of God united.

Time is short. As the Lord's return approaches, we should dedicate ourselves fully to serving Christ, reject sin, confront it in our lives, and stay united. Maintain your commitment to the church and avoid trying to handle life on your own outside of it.

Matthew 18:14, In the same way, it is not the will of your Father in heaven that one of these little ones perish. You were separated from the flock because of sin, but God sent the greatest missionary from heaven. He came from heaven, lived perfectly, died for your sins, and rose from the dead. Through the Holy Spirit's power, He sought you out and reconciled you to the Father. He pursued you and restored your relationship with God, so why shouldn't we do the same for others?

Chapter 42

Prayer

Lord God, I ask that the weight of the world's burdens press heavily on your sons' and daughters' hearts and souls. Please pour out a pastoral spirit within us so we genuinely care for our brothers and sisters. Please help us to stop looking down on them or hating them unnecessarily. Father, I pray that with a shepherd's love, we do everything possible to combat sin, maintain childlike faith, stay humble, and keep our community united. Bring back the wanderers—our prodigal sons and daughters who are part of this family. Rescue those lost in darkness—save sons and daughters in darkness—by the power of our Lord and Savior, Jesus Christ.

CHAPTER 43

CHURCH

Christ provides a framework for resolving conflicts within the community. Note the word "if"—it shows that in the biblical community, there's always a possibility of being deeply hurt by someone inside the church. The Lord corrects the misconception that joining or being part of a church guarantees you'll never be hurt. Many of us attend gatherings, get involved, and because we expect others to be holy, we believe we can stay for weeks, months, or years without experiencing pain. This mindset reflects an American view of the church, not a biblical one. Jesus warned us, even before the church's founding, that as long as we are in community with believers, there's always a risk of being wounded by someone's sin against us.

Matthew 18:15, "If your brother sins against you, go tell him his fault, between him and you alone. If he listens to you, you have won your brother."

The word 'go' calls for immediate action. Don't remain passive or indifferent about your pain. If you're awake at night feeling upset over what someone did or is doing to you, the Lord is giving you permission to go and speak with that brother or sister. Ignoring it can result in resentment, unforgiveness, and ongoing pain, letting these feelings intensify.

If the Lord instructed us to confront anyone every time we feel annoyed, we wouldn't last long. Feeling annoyed doesn't necessarily mean we need to address it by talking to someone. Instead, maturity teaches us to go to our prayer space when specific issues upset us. When you feel offended or frustrated, turn to prayer. Only immature believers ignore this. God always responds when you experience emotions caused by others. As we grow, we learn to manage these feelings more effectively.

The Lord did not design the church to be in ongoing conflict each week. He discusses situations where church members sin against you collectively. The Lord allows you to handle these issues directly. If you can pray when others wrong you and then move on, praise God for that. The Lord provides us with grace to manage healthy conflicts among ourselves.

The Lord never guaranteed that you wouldn't face hurt or offenses from someone in the church. While many expect Christians to be perfect, the reality is that others may always be tempted to hurt you. Jesus recommended honest dialogue—sharing your feelings, tears, and the pain you've endured. It's essential to communicate your experiences to the person involved. Some individuals have hearts so troubled that they thrive on chaos. They tend to extend conflicts, hold onto grudges, and cause self-inflicted harm. Instead of resolving these tensions, many bottled up their emotions, leading to internal suffering.

Approaching someone with humility and love, while sharing your feelings of hurt—something they might not even realize you're experiencing—can foster healing and reconciliation. This aligns with Jesus' teachings on relationship restoration. Offering grace and keeping peace are vital for your well-being. Some individuals refuse to listen because they are immature, prideful, insecure, or arrogant. No matter how kind and gentle you are when addressing their sins, you'll often see their true character. If they have good character, they'll usually listen if you speak in love, humility, and godliness. But if they lack love and integrity, they may continue causing drama. Do you know what the Lord advises us to do in such cases?

Matthew 18:16, But if he won't listen, take one or two others with you, so that by the testimony of two or three witnesses every fact may be established.

The Lord emphasizes that if someone sins against you within the church, it's a serious and painful matter—it wounds you. You should first approach that brother or sister privately. If you succeed in reconciling, the issue is settled. However, if they refuse to listen, the Lord cares deeply about unity among His followers. He advises that if initial efforts fail, you should bring two or three others and try again. The second approach involves someone objective, perhaps more authoritative, mature, or spiritually wise. The goal is that if your words alone don't persuade, these others might be able to communicate something that you couldn't, increasing the chances of resolution.

99% of all church conflicts should end right there.

Matthew 18:17, *If he doesn't pay attention to them, tell the church, let him be like a gentile, and a tax collector to you.*

God knows his heart—he understands it is wicked and full of sin. Because of His love, the Lord desires him to repent. He wants you to help him change, but if we enable him to remain in sin, he will never be transformed. Therefore, love instructs us to distance ourselves from him.

The criteria for church discipline are unclear because the scriptures do not explicitly mention adults; they only refer to believers as "children of God," and disobedient children need correction. Is there any evidence that they listen to his words after the Lord is gone? Paul, an apostle who was once a murderer and became a Christian, addresses a disorderly church filled with talented yet impulsive individuals, as seen in **1 Corinthians 5:1-5.**

Paul asks whether you are arrogant or if you are more inclined to mourn. Your heart should be broken over the sin of this brother who has caused the downfall of his father's wife. Shouldn't your heart be grieved to see how this young man is destroying a family and harming the church?

I love Jesus and have a personal relationship with Him, but I don't depend solely on the church. If the church represents His body, then how can you truly love Him? The New Testament offers no doctrine that supports a solo approach. He invites all His followers to be part of a community because His greatest work in us happens through communal sanctification—by sharing life, coaching, loving, disciplining, training, breaking down barriers, building up, and comforting one another. Many Christians on social media say, "We love God but don't need the church," but this is a misconception.

Jesus warns that unrepentant individuals might find their prayers attracting the devil's influence. Why? Because we genuinely care about you—it's better to endure the pain of your sins now than to die and face eternal separation from God. Many people are living, preaching, serving, and leading while sinning, acting on their desires, which puts many of us at risk of eternal separation from God.

Paul also writes about this in **2 Corinthians 2:5-10,** *If anyone has caused pain, he has caused pain not so much to me but to some degree-not to exaggerate-to all of you. This punishment by the majority is sufficient for that person. As a result, you should instead forgive and comfort him. Otherwise, he may be overwhelmed by excessive grief. Therefore I urge you to reaffirm your love to him. I wrote for this purpose: to test your character to see if you are obedient in everything. Anyone you forgive, I do too. For what I have forgiven-if I have forgiven anything it is for your benefit in the presence of Christ.*

I'm returning to where I belong to apologize. Please invite me back into the fellowship. All I want is to be loved and accepted again. The Lord understood that implementing this level of church discipline would be a challenging task. It would not be simple; it could be stressful for the leadership team.

Matthew 18:18, Truly I tell you, Whatever you bind on earth will have been bound in heaven, and whatever you loose on earth will have been loosed in heaven. This passage addresses church discipline and what the Lord instructs leaders to do. If you remove someone described as 'bind', I will support your decision from heaven. Conversely, if you restore that person by 'inviting' them back into fellowship – I will also support your decision from heaven.

No one is escaping accountability. The Lord approves your choice when it is made rightly — righteous, holy, and aligned with my teachings. **Matthew 18:19-20,** Again, truly I tell you, if 2 of you on earth agree about any matter that you pray for, it will be done for you by my Father in heaven. For where two or three are gathered together in my name, I am there among them.

You're praying to the Lord, asking Him to intervene for that person: to save, deliver, open their eyes, help them feel Your love, and bring them back. Request their repentance, knowing that if you cry out for someone in a sinful, unrepentant, rebellious state, God will hear from heaven and act. God is love, and He does not call us to confrontations or battles. Instead, He invites us to acts of love. We are not meant to be fighting brothers and sisters, but to seek reconciliation. He doesn't want us to abandon people but to fight to protect the community of saints.

Recall Jesus' words: He set an example because we sinned against God. We were born in sin and have often sinned. The law could have abandoned us in sin, but it didn't. Instead, Jesus, guided by the Holy Spirit, pursued us, leaving the 99 to confront us with conviction and attempts to restore us to the Father.

Jesus came, lived, and died, using the Holy Spirit to bring you to the cross, not to keep you in sin. Instead of condemning you, He calls you back to reconciliation with the Father. Since you are reconciled, He also encourages you to reconcile with others. Aim to love one another deeply, because love covers a multitude of sins.

Chapter 44

Prayer

Heavenly Father, we thank you for the strength and truth of your word. We value your holy teachings, wisdom, and brilliance. I pray that the church worldwide turns away from secular humanistic doctrines. Instead, may we abandon the ways of the world and embrace your word, teachings, and exaltations—focusing on you, Lord, in all things. I ask for a revival of repentance to sweep through this nation in the name of your Son. Touch the hearts and minds of your children regarding the name of Jesus, praying that today, prison doors open, shackles are broken, and fall off. Ignite and stir our hearts, for the end is near. Help us share your truth with others and love as you love us. In Jesus' name. Amen.

CHAPTER 45

BE FREE

After accepting salvation through the Lord Jesus Christ, the greatest gift from God is the gift of relationships. We have gathered a collection of treasured memories—laughter, trips, tears of joy—and these blessings come through our connections. They open doors, offer shoulders to cry on, and attentive ears. Throughout life, we also face pain and sorrow within our relationships.

Jesus teaches in **Matthew 18** that we should not let our hearts be consumed with the pursuit of glory, affirmation, power, or prestige. Instead, He emphasizes that true greatness is rooted in humility. Entering the Kingdom requires humility in our relationships with others, treating them as if we are interacting with Christ himself. The passage also stresses the importance of avoiding causing others to stumble or fall into sin. When we recognize destructive sin patterns in ourselves, we are guided to protect ourselves and others by eliminating those sinful behaviors. It also reminds us not to look down on fellow believers but to value their worth, even if we don't naturally feel a connection. Lastly, it teaches that when a brother or sister goes astray, we should leave the majority and seek out the one to bring them back.

Matthew 18:21, *Then Peter approached him and asked, "Lord, how many times must I forgive my brother or sister who sins against me? As many as seven times?"* The Lord knows there are pains inflicted on us by friends, former spouses, groups, or mentors. Some wounds are so deep that I wonder if I can keep forgiving over and over again. I'm not sure if I have that capacity. **Matthew 18:21,** "I tell you, not as many as seven," Jesus replied, "but seventy times seven."

Peter struggles with forgiveness. Although forgiveness was only briefly addressed in the 1st century, the Lord later transformed that teaching. The Lord doesn't ask us to keep track of how many times we forgive someone. Instead, we should keep forgiving those who hurt us without keeping a count. Forgiveness can be tough, especially when we find ourselves forgiving the same person repeatedly—whether it's after divorce, abuse (physical or mental), childhood trauma, abandonment, or rejection. No matter the circumstances, we know it's difficult, but the Lord still calls us to forgive.

Forgiving others when they hurt us isn't easy in our natural state. From my own experience, my first reaction is usually not forgiveness; instead, I often feel pain, tears, and heartbreak, holding onto that person until I can respond. The Lord understands our human nature and knows that, in our weakness, this teaching can be difficult for us.

Many of us have held onto unforgiveness in our hearts. I understand how difficult that can be, and the Lord knows it, too. In His mercy, God tells Peter a parable and a hidden story, teaching him a lesson and encouraging grace and strength so he can obey. The longer you live, the more likely someone will hurt you deeply enough to make forgiveness seem impossible. Still, the Lord gives us the inner strength to respond wisely to those who cause us pain.

As Christians, we often hope for an apology, but we might never get one from someone outside our spiritual authority. It is important not to expect too much from those not submitted to the Lord Jesus Christ. This teaching is meant for Kingdom believers. The Lord speaks to us—His followers—calling you a Christian, not an atheist or agnostic.

Matthew 18:26-27, "At this, the servant fell face down before him and said, 'Be patient with me, and I will pay you everything.' Then the master of that servant had compassion, released him, and forgave him the loan." This servant symbolizes everyone who is saved—those who have called out to God for forgiveness. The Lord hears your cry, welcomes you into His Kingdom, grants you His Spirit, and forgives your sins. Initially, you were headed toward damnation, but God responded to your plea, canceling a debt you couldn't pay. We are born in sin, commit sins, and anyone who dies in sin is separated from God forever, with hell as their eternal home. Yet, for those who ask, 'God, forgive me for my sins,' and if the Lord hears, He cancels that debt, makes you His child, and sets you free.

Even those of us who have repeatedly received God's grace still deserve His wrath. Some believe God owes them His grace, but in reality, He owes them nothing but judgment. Yet, you woke up this morning, alert and blessed in many ways; what you truly deserve is wrath. The Lord explained to all my children who have been forgiven and received His grace that we are like servants burdened with an unpayable debt. However, He listened to your prayers, saw your humility, and chose to cancel that debt. He is showcasing God's heart toward saved humans for you to see, exemplifying grace, forgiveness, and mercy.

Reference: Matthew 18:28-34

The man forgiven of his debt quickly forgets his forgiveness, much like us at times. Your parent, spouse, abuser, church member who slandered you, child who cursed you, or friend who betrayed you—how fast we forget when we've been forgiven. The same servant then finds someone who owes him a small debt and chokes him. Is that what you said? He chokes him. That's vengeance. When we're hurt, our first instinct isn't grace but vengeance—we close our hearts to those seeking mercy. This behavior is immoral, ungodly, hypocritical, and many of us, myself included, have been guilty of it.

When you notice a brother or sister struggling with sin, pray to the Father and share your concerns. Show God that you care about their freedom and ask for His help to lift any burdens they carry. This demonstrates love and concern. Holding onto unforgiveness keeps you trapped in internal punishment and steals peace from your soul. Just as the Lord imprisoned the servant who couldn't repay his debt—giving him a life sentence unless he repented—this highlights the consequences of unforgiveness. Although it may seem the Lord isn't that harsh, Jesus included **chapter 35** to emphasize this.

Matthew 18:35, So also my heavenly Father will do to you unless every one of you forgives his brother or sister from your heart. The Lord says that if you refuse to forgive, divine punishment will follow until you release that person. This could be your mother or father who caused you pain. True peace is only achievable once you decide to forgive and let go. I understand that this isn't easy—think of it this way: you don't forgive others just for them; you do it to protect yourself. Sometimes, forgiving someone might feel like you're losing control or a part of yourself.

They betrayed you, destroyed your marriage, fractured your family, hurt you, and caused tears that can never be replaced. Those moments and tears can never be recovered. Some may never even have the chance to apologize; you can't go back. The lesson from the Lord is that forgiveness isn't about them, but about your freedom. It's time to break free from the emotional trap and start truly living again. Joy will come after the pain. This isn't the Lord telling you to be a doormat or to excuse sin. Instead, it's a reminder that He cares deeply about your freedom and wants you to live a life rich with limitless forgiveness. When you forgive others, you're not doing it for them—you're doing it for you.

Let go of everyone you've been holding in your heart for years or decades. You're still stuck in that season; He wants you to release them. Every time you see me, it reminds you of the cross and Christ's sacrifice. On the cross, He completely paid your debt of sin. He says, "Now see what I did for you on the cross." Turn away from that and keep releasing others in the same way. Is Christ's blood sufficient? It may require patience, but deciding to release is the initial step towards healing.

CHAPTER 46

PRAYER

Dear Heavenly Father, I rely on your power to declare the truths of your sacred scriptures. Please pour out upon us a spirit of conviction, repentance, and awakening. Meet us where we are and challenge us through your word; let it resonate deeply within us, revealing anything that doesn't reflect you. Lord, draw us closer to you and inspire us to go beyond this moment. We long to hear your voice from heaven and ask you to transform our hearts and minds today. I pray for unbelievers to experience a stirring within their souls. Open their ears and eyes, ignite their hearts, and move us all as you send divine revelation from heaven. I pray all this in your precious Son, Jesus. Amen.

CHAPTER 47

RELATIONSHIPS

Marriage

Marriage is more than just a covenant between a man and a woman; it also represents Christ and the church. Although conflicts can happen in the earthly realm, spiritually, every visible biblical union serves as a source of frustration for the devil. He sees a reflection of Christ and the church and, using deception and lies, attacks marriage—trying to cut, damage, distort, or destroy it in any way he can.

Many married couples often face conflicts later in their relationships. Statistics show that half of all marriages, including church marriages, end in divorce. It seems that sustaining marriage in our society is difficult, but this isn't because people are inherently evil. Instead, much of the challenge comes from an adversary who opposes marriage. Society is trying to redefine marriage, which is seen as satanic. Some people dishonor marriage, demonstrating satanic tendencies. Others approach marriage in opposition to God, and all these actions are considered satanic.

Divorce

Matthew 19:3, Some Pharisees approached him to test him. They asked, ***"Is it lawful for a man to divorce his wife on any grounds?"*** These Pharisees test Jesus with a question, indicating their motives are not genuine; they want to trap Him in a theological debate. As followers of Christ, it's essential to be discerning in our conversations and interactions. Not everyone who speaks to us has good intentions, not everyone seeking friendship is sincere, and not every theological discussion is honest.

Moses recorded this law from God in **Deuteronomy 24:1-3**. *He allows divorce to protect women and prevent their abuse. Historically, men could divorce for any reason, and by Jesus' time, respect for marriage had significantly diminished.* You live in a culture where divorce occurs frequently. I'm not condemning justified divorces; instead, I note that when Jesus discussed this topic, he spoke to men in a society where trivial divorces were common.

Matthew 19:4, "Haven't you read," he replied, "that he who created them in the beginning made them male and female."

Jesus does not directly answer the divorce question; instead, he points them back to God's word. Men and women dismiss the false idea in the church that non-binary gender exists. However, Christians continue to like these people's social media posts because their preferences outweigh God's word. There are only two pronouns and two genders. Jesus stated he created them as male and female. **Matthew 19:5-6,** And he also said, 'For this reason A man will leave his father and mother and be joined to his wife, and the two will become one flesh.' So they are no longer 2, but one flesh. Therefore, what God has joined together, let no one separate.

The Lord is guiding us to return to the Bible's teachings. In God's original plan, marriage is a covenant between one man and one woman. He desires married couples to be closely linked through communication, sharing, forgiveness, and maintaining a strong bond. Marriage is a union where a man and a woman become one flesh, with sexual intimacy kept within this covenant to ensure a firm union. This prevents us from forming emotional or mental ties with others outside the marriage, which can often cause turmoil.

We should not judge people with same-sex attraction because, in Genesis 1 and 2, Adam and Eve were in a perfect state before rebelling against God. Sin has since corrupted marriage, leading to ongoing conflicts and struggles for thousands of years. Overcoming sinful tendencies is difficult, especially as society continues to redefine marriage. Marriage's challenges are not because of an evil spouse, but because everyone is affected by sin. God's original plan was that any two people who marry will never part until one dies. This is God revealing to the Pharisees, in their argument, what God's original design was.

They are similar to us in that they also prioritize their preferences over God's truth, as we sometimes do. Instead of accepting reality and letting it change us, we often come up with reasons to reject God's truth inwardly. Instead, we should allow God's truth to challenge and influence us. It is important to let God address issues within our hearts.

This is God revealing to the Pharisees, in their argument, what God's original design was. In **Matthew 19:7, *"Why then,"* they asked him, *"did Moses command us to give divorce papers and to send her away?"* Matthew 19:8-9,** He told them, "Moses permitted you to divorce your wives because of the hardness of your hearts, but it was not like that from the beginning. I tell you, whoever divorces his wife, except for sexual immorality, and marries another commits adultery."

The Lord speaks directly about the situation related to the question He received. God's original plan for humanity, based on His wisdom, was that following

His guidance would lead to the best life. However, we now realize that this is more complex because, at that time, the couple was perfect. Today, we see that marriage takes place within a sinful world. This understanding makes it more challenging, which is why Scripture consistently provides teachings on marriage to help men and women navigate their flesh while dealing with sin.

Matthew 19:10 His Disciples said to him, *"If the relationship of a man whose wife is like this, it's better not to marry."* They recognize the seriousness of God's original intention for marriage. Understanding that marriage is sacred before God, established as an eternal covenant until death, they see it as something not to be taken lightly or misused. Given the importance of marriage in God's view, they consider that remaining single could be a preferable choice.

Being Single

Matthew 19:11-12, He responded, "Not everyone can accept this saying, but only those to whom it has been given. For there are eunuchs who were born that way from their mother's womb, there are eunuchs who were made by men, and there are eunuchs who have made themselves that way because of the Kingdom of heaven. The one who is able to accept it should accept it."

The Lord affirmed the worth of singleness, clarifying that it is not a curse and that marriage isn't the ultimate aim. In biblical times, eunuchs—men castrated to avoid temptation from women and serve kings—were used to demonstrate that some people are born as eunuchs or choose to become one to serve the Lord without the distraction of a spouse. While God praises singleness, societal pressures still encourage everyone to marry.

For married individuals, the covenant you share is sacred, and the Lord wants you to actively uphold it, as it represents Christ's relationship with the church. If you're single, see it as a divine calling that Jesus has special purposes for. This does not mean you are less of a man or woman; instead, the Lord may want you all to Himself for a time.

No matter your circumstances, we are all regarded as married. The Son of God, who referred to Himself as a groom, formed a relationship with us. He founded the church, His bride, and proclaimed Himself married to her eternally. Despite our betrayals—such as seeking other lovers, and exhibiting rudeness, cruelty, rebellion, and disobedience—He has never granted a divorce. He sealed your marriage with His blood and remains devoted to you forever. Good.

The one who came, lived, died, rose, married us, and placed a ring on—such a ring will never be removed. For married couples, may the Lord guide us. For those who are divorced, grace will be given. And for single individuals, you may come to see it as God's will for you, at least for now.

I pray that all Americans will uphold and protect the sanctity of the church's marriage covenant. I lift up couples facing marital struggles and those who have endured painful divorces. I also pray for singles, asking that they remain pure until their appointed time for marriage—or stay single if that is God's plan. Help us look beyond cultural opinions to honor you according to your Word. I ask this in the name of our Lord and Savior, Jesus Christ. Amen.

CHAPTER 48

PRAYER

Dear Heavenly Father, awaken your children and breathe upon them now. I pray they gain a biblical understanding that time is short, fulfillment is near, and they should be motivated to serve you. Help them value the Kingdom and develop a longing to surrender fully to you. Free them from idolatry, self-worship, and false gods. Show them how wonderfully you have blessed them through salvation, providing all they need for life and godliness. Nothing is more precious than your Son, and we often take that for granted. May this message ignite a fire in their hearts and fill them with the joy of the Kingdom. Lord, allow them to feel a sense of purpose and significance; may their focus be on you and your Kingdom. I pray this in your precious name, Jesus Christ. Amen.

CHAPTER 49

GIVING IT ALL UP

Some non-believers think they need to fix their lives first before coming to God in faith. Many religious people believe they can earn God's approval through good deeds and actions, as if their behavior can truly make them righteous. This way of thinking is restrictive and draining. **Matthew 19:16-17,** Just then, someone came up and asked, "Teacher, what good must I do to have eternal life?" "Why do you ask me about what is good?" he said to him. "There is only one who is good. If you want to enter into life, keep the commandments." The word 'if' here functions as a clause. He links 'if' to eternal life, implying there is a cost to entering heaven.

Jesus does two things here: He corrects the man and then teaches him. First, He corrects by asking, "Why do you call me good?" He waits for a reply, but none is given at that moment. Jesus is suggesting that no human is morally perfect or truly good, as no one possesses absolute goodness.

Paul writes to the church in Rome, recognizing that everyone has fallen short and sinned, and is without God's glory. He explains that no person can reach moral perfection. When individuals claim they are good enough for heaven, they are mistaken because Christ teaches that nobody is morally perfect or can earn salvation. He emphasizes that only God is perfect, referencing Himself, the Father, and the Holy Spirit.

At funerals, preachers often offer false comfort by claiming everyone in a casket is destined for heaven. They imply that all Americans who pass away are in a better place, assuming heaven is a guaranteed afterlife. More than 75% of Americans believe the deceased go to heaven automatically. In the U.S., we tend to think death results in heaven without considering that some may not reach it. To ease our guilt, we often insist that all who die are in a better place, regardless of their actions.

If you know someone who doesn't know Jesus as their Lord and Savior, pray that they come to this knowledge before it's too late. Not everyone is in a good state now. Jesus said that believing in Him results in eternal life, which suggests that entering eternity involves making a choice or accepting a cost. Many Americans don't think much about eternal life, and many Christians are too focused on leveraging their position for personal benefit.

Commandments

Matthew 19:18, "Which ones?" he asked him. Jesus answered: Do not murder; do not commit adultery; do not steal; do not bear false witness; honor your father and your mother; and love your neighbor as yourself. The Lord refers to six commandments, but leaves out some elements. He doesn't say, "God loves you" or mention grace. Nor does he suggest, "Invite Jesus into your heart" or emphasize God's need for him. Instead, he avoids common American gospel phrases and delivers God's message through moral commandments, providing the seeker with the six Commandments.

The Lord presents six commandments but leaves out the others. He doesn't say, "God loves you" or mention grace. Nor does he encourage, "Invite Jesus into your heart," or emphasize God's need for him. Instead, he sidesteps typical American gospel methods and communicates God's message through moral commandments, giving the seeker the six Commandments.

Some individuals believe they have earned God's favor through actions such as attending church and giving tithes and offerings. They are people across the country who, judging by their outward displays of piety, consider themselves justified in God's eyes.

Matthew 19:21, "If you want to be perfect," Jesus said to him, "go sell your belongings and give to the poor, and you will have treasure in heaven. Then come, follow me."

The Lord reveals the true path to sharing the gospel. Entry into heaven requires perfection—morally, as perfect as God. This raises the question: who can earn their way into heaven? No one. Therefore, those of us saved and on our way to heaven should steer clear of pride or arrogance about our salvation. We must stop boasting about our talents, gifts, or anything else we believe has earned us God's favor. Instead, our only reason to boast is the cross and Christ's work, because that's all we can rely on.

I encourage you to love and cherish Christ, making Him the focus of your heart, mind, and home. Love Him completely, for if you're saved and destined for heaven, it is through His work and righteousness covering you—that's the reason to love Him. Our pride should solely be in Christ's work, not in our talents like communication, singing, administration, or leadership, which might tempt us to think, "That's why God saved me." The truth is, outside of Christ, we are nothing. Our only offering to God is Christ's righteousness. Heaven's standard is—listen— perfection, moral perfection. Since sin cannot be in God's presence, moral perfection is vital. As we are not morally perfect, we must be clothed in someone else's moral perfection.

Remember that we are clothed in Christ. When the devil accuses you, remind him that Christ protects you. We often associate righteousness with temporary, worldly, or legalistic things—yet true righteousness comes from faith in Christ alone. Jesus offers the greatest invitation anyone will ever receive: **'Come and follow me.'** No invitation is greater. He knows our insecurities, brokenness, and past struggles, yet He still invites us. When He says **'Come,'** He fully understands what He is accepting. Nothing in you surprises Him.

Matthew 19:22, *When the young man heard that, he went away grieving, because he had many possessions.*

This man chose not to follow Jesus. Unlike us, who haven't personally seen Him, imagine standing before Christ, the incarnate God, and refusing His invitation— an opportunity of immense importance. The law revealed that he was violating the first commandment: "You shall love the Lord your God and have no other gods before Him." His disobedience was internal. Because of that idolatry in his heart, he would be separated from God forever. To this man, whose greatest priority was his wealth, the Lord says, "You are not perfect. Sell that idol, then come and follow me." He missed the chance to walk with Christ because his wealth was more important than the call.

People with many possessions often struggle to enter the Kingdom because they rely on their wealth and self-sufficiency. As a result, the wealthy may think they don't need God, believing their money will always guarantee comfort. Since our gospel outreach can sometimes be ineffective, we often approach wealthy individuals by saying, **"Jesus will improve your life,"** which is a weak message. They may see this as, **"I don't need God because my life is already good."** Therefore, the Lord did not simply say to the wealthy man, "God loves you and offers grace," but instead addressed his sin, because wealth alone cannot buy righteousness.

Matthew 19:23-24, Jesus said to his disciples, *"Truly I tell you, it will be hard for a rich person to enter the Kingdom of heaven. Again I tell you, it is easier for a camel to go through the eye of a needle than for a rich person to enter the Kingdom of God."* The Greek word 'needle' denotes a sewing needle with a tiny eye. Jesus describes that entering heaven cannot be achieved through personal effort, similar to how it is impossible to pass an animal through the eye of a sewing needle.

Matthew 19:25, *When the disciples heard this, they were utterly astonished and asked, "Then who can be saved?"* In the 1st century, it was commonly believed that God blessed the wealthy. Consequently, it was reasoned that if a wealthy individual couldn't gain entry, then no one else could. **Matthew 19:26-27,** Jesus looked at them and said, "With man this is impossible, but with God all things are possible." Then Peter responded to him, "See, we have left everything and followed you. So what will there be for us?"

Matthew 19-28-30, Jesus said to them, "Truly I tell you, in the renewal of all things, when the Son of Man sits on his glorious throne, you who have followed me will also sit on twelve thrones, judging the twelve tribes of Israel. And everyone who has left houses or brothers or sisters or fathers or mothers or children or fields because of my name will receive a hundred times more and will inherit eternal life. But many who are first will be last, and the last first."

This message is for believers who feel they have sacrificed everything for the Lord but don't seem to prosper like the wicked. It's a valid concern—perhaps you reach some goals, but what if you don't? The Lord shifts the focus for His followers: the reward isn't just immediate but also eternal. What do we gain by following Christ through suffering? The answer is straightforward: if you have Him, you gain eternal life. Those who are comfortable now may end up last, and some might not enter at all, while those who endure suffering will be first. A significant reversal awaits the judgment.

Revelation 20:11-15

Is eternity not enough for you? Do you reject Christ? Do you believe salvation is insufficient? Those not written in the book of life are thrown into the lake of fire, where they burn forever. For those of us who want eternity with the Father and our name in the book of life, **Revelation 21:6-8, *Then he said to me, "It is done! I am the Alpha and the Omega, the beginning and the end. I will freely give to the*** *thirsty from the spring of the water of life. The one who conquers will inherit these things, and I will be his God, and he will be my son. But the cowards, faithless, detestable, murderers, sexually immoral, sorcerers, idolaters, and all liars- their share will be in the lake that burns with fire and sulfur, which is the second death.*

The ultimate reward for our suffering and effort is eternity. We are called to share the gospel both as a community and individually. Those who dedicate their lives and sacrifice everything for Christ, abandoning all to follow Him, will receive the crown they humbly place at His feet.

CHAPTER 50

PRAYER

Heavenly Father, I come to you now, praying that you draw us closer to yourself through your word. Help us to look beyond our usual reading of the Scriptures and marvel at your truth, seeing Christ as central to every verse. In our weakness, we depend on your strength. May we long for a deeper relationship with you. I ask that you fill us with encouragement and inspiration, ignite passion in all your children's hearts, and fill us with a spirit of evangelism. Let the burden of the world weigh heavily on us and move us through your truth. I pray this in the name of your precious Son, Jesus. Amen.

CHAPTER 51

ALL FOR YOU!

Matthew 20:17-19, While going up to Jerusalem, Jesus took the twelve disciples aside privately and said to them on the way, "See, we are going up to Jerusalem. The Son of Man will be handed over to the chief priests and scribes, and they will condemn him to death. They will hand him over to the Gentiles to be mocked, flogged, and crucified, and on the third day he will be raised."

Flogging was an extremely harsh punishment. The person delivering it used a whip called the cat of nine tails, which was essentially a pole with multiple leather straps attached. Each strap featured a metal or bone end. When you struck someone with that whip, it could pierce the skin, and upon pulling it away, it would tear flesh from the person. Remember that He suffered for your sins and mine.

Therefore, we should avoid loving sin and instead develop a strong dislike for it. When sin appears in our lives, the church, or society, it should bring us sadness. We ought to mourn sin in our personal lives, the church, America, and the whole country. Sin carries a heavy price because of the cost it demands. As followers of Christ, we must not only focus on Jesus' suffering on the cross but also avoid turning to sin.

Though we may stumble and sin, we should not harbor love for sin in our hearts. Instead, we are called to despise sin, iniquity, and anything that grieves God's heart. When sin causes us pain and leaves us broken, we should consistently turn back to Him in repentance. For those whose names are written in the book of life, hope goes beyond death. One day, we will leave this damaged body behind, and others will mourn the shell that once held us. However, we ask that your mourning not last long, as we have left this earthly form and entered into God's presence.

Our perspective changes when we view God's presence not just as a source of blessings but as the ultimate way to encounter Him. The main goal of prayer is to meet Christ face-to-face. This involves entering His presence, sometimes sitting with Him, loving Him, and experiencing His love in return. I suggest that those who find prayer difficult try listening to worship music or instrumental worship and sit in His presence. Imagine Him being exalted and glorified, visualize fire in His eyes, and remind yourself that He is returning for you. Practice quietly sitting with Him, contemplating His position on the throne, and gradually feel more at ease in His presence. In tough times, remember how He has supported you through previous hardships. Open your heart and begin pouring out your feelings to Him.

Paul told the church at Corinth that our spiritual weapons are not physical but powerful in God for demolishing strongholds. We should capture wrong thoughts, tear them down, bring them into obedience to Christ, and continually replace them with the thoughts from God's word. **2Corinthians 10:3-4,** *For although we live in the flesh, we do not wage war according to the flesh, since the weapons of our warfare are not of the flesh, but are powerful through God for the demolition of strongholds. We demolish arguments.* Remember that not all thoughts come from you, as the devil, who is a liar, is at work. The same devil, who attempted to spark conflict in Jesus's heart after His 40-day fast in the wilderness, also aims to cause unrest in our hearts and minds. Although the battle is real, we must learn how to resist.

Matthew 20:20-21, Then the mother of Zebedee's sons approached him with her sons. She knelt down to ask him for something. "What do you want?" he asked her. *"Promise,"* she said to him, *"that these two sons of mine may sit, one on your right and the other on your left, in your kingdom."*

This is Salome, the mother of James and John. She was concerned about her sons' glory while Jesus spoke about suffering.

Matthew 20:22-23, Jesus answered, "You don't know what you're asking. Are you able to drink the cup that I'm about to drink?" ***"We are able,"*** they said to him. He told them, "You will indeed drink my cup, but to sit at my right and left is not mine to give; instead, it is for those for whom it has been prepared by my Father."

Jesus discusses his suffering and the idea of sharing the same cup. He also notes that James and John's mother's desires do not align with God's will. We often do similar things for our children, trying to guide them in ways that might not match God's plan. Good parenting involves not just discipline but also helping children follow God's path. Sometimes, suffering leads us to reflect on Christ's suffering for us. This hardship is temporary and minor, especially when compared to the glory that awaits. When we suffer, we want to be free of it, but He uses these experiences to teach us lessons before taking away the pain.

To achieve greatness, aim to be a great servant. Keep praying persistently, especially during tough times. Instead of praying just once or ten times, consistently ask the Lord for His strength, grace, mercy, or guidance. He wants you to depend on Him, work with Him, and continue praying. This gives hope that you can also recover what might be lost — you're not beyond repair.

If you feel distant from God, remember you have the power to restore your relationship with Him. When your prayers seem unheard, reconnect through faith. God is always ready to intervene in your life, showing lasting mercy and quick forgiveness. He is slow to anger and patiently waits for you to return to His loving embrace. Often, the simplest prayer is, "Lord, have mercy on me." God understands when you're facing hardships. He calls out, 'My son, my daughter, you are my beloved.' Even if you're unsure about yourself, His love remains constant. Keep faith.

Sometimes, we feel overwhelmed by self-loathing and harsh self-criticism, believing we're always failing. This often stems from insecurities that intensify when we lack affirmation or do not receive praise, such as "Well done" or "You did a good job." When you're spiritually lost, you can restore your balance by crying out, "Lord, have mercy on me.' That simple prayer is enough. Remember, the Lord Jesus lived, died, and rose again entirely for you.

A Note From The Author

Now that you've finished this book, I hope it has provided you with insights into how we should live as Christians and children of God. It's crucial to do more than say you'll pray for someone — actually lift them in prayer. Be passionate about sharing the gospel widely and never feel ashamed of our Lord and Savior, Jesus Christ. He deserves our praise, and we must seek out His lost children, as He commands when He says, **"Proclaim Me."**

Mark 16:15, "Go into **all the world and preach the gospel to all creation.**"

About The Author

Crystal Cattabriga is an award-winning author of Christian and spiritual books.

Her work includes Saving Bobby, which won her a Readers' Favorite gold medal. Seek Me (a finalist in the National Indie Excellence Awards. She was born in Massachusetts, where her love and passion for writing came from when she was a child. As a young child, she spent most of her time reading Beatrice Potter books and anything else she could get her hands on in her local library, imagining stories that took her to faraway places. Creating stories of love and hope with a sprinkle of Jesus is exactly what she enjoys. One act of kindness goes a long way in a world with so much darkness. She and her family left city life years ago, finding their new life in the North Georgia mountains.

Romans 12:2, *"Do not conform to this age, but be transformed by the renewing of your mind, so that you discern what is the good, pleasing, and perfect will of God."*

Social Media

TikTok- Facebook- Instagram